"After Lewis Smedes wrote his classic text on forgiveness, what else could be said? I was wrong. Randall O'Brien's *Set Free by Forgiveness* is fresh, informative, inspiring, and insightful. Reflected in its pages are practical words from a pastor, biblical depth from a theologian, and a perceptive analysis of the human condition by a wise teacher. O'Brien opens long-closed doors in all of us, pointing the way to healing and the peace of forgiveness."

Joe E. Trull, editor, *Christian Ethics Today*

"Forgiveness is central to our faith, essential to our lives, and (too often) nearly impossible to give or to receive. Randall O'Brien delivers a powerful combination of biblical scholarship, psychological insight, and practical wisdom about why and how to forgive ourselves, others, and God. If you want to be freed from the pain of holding on to your wounds, then this book is a must read for you."

Steve Wells, senior pastor, South Main Baptist Church, Houston, Texas

"Written by one of America's best storytellers, this book artfully combines accessible prose with powerful stories, both of which are Randall O'Brien's hallmarks. *Set Free by Forgiveness* also makes a wider contribution by clarifying the differences between topics like forgiveness and justice, between forgiveness and reconciliation. O'Brien engages a wide range of literature and produces a work that is clear, constructive, and compelling."

D. Michael Lindsay, Harold W. Dodds Fellow, department of sociology, Princeton University

"'Forgiveness happens to the person doing it; it may or may not affect the person who hurt you.' This insightful and freeing view of forgiveness is a taste of the wisdom Randall O'Brien offers in *Set Free by Forgiveness*. He not only points to the power of forgiveness, but he provides a map to guide Christians in the demanding discipline of forgiveness, a discipline he recognizes is truly impossible without the grace of God. Moreover, O'Brien helps readers admit that sometimes forgiving those who have wronged us is less demanding than admitting that we need to forgive God for injustice we do not understand and, ultimately, to forgive ourselves for the sin that has misshapen our lives and hurt those we love. With many compelling stories and pithy sayings, O'Brien applies theological truths to everyday life in ways that encourage readers to claim the grace of God's forgiveness for self and others. *Set Free by Forgiveness* will be grace in the lives of individual readers and will serve as an excellent book to read together in church groups and in self-help groups of those who have suffered or have caused suffering in the many ways we hurt one another in family and community life."

Diana R. Garland, dean, School of Social Work, and director, Center for Family and Community Ministries, Baylor University

SET FREE BY
Forgiveness

SET FREE BY
Forgiveness

The Way to Peace and Healing

Randall O'Brien

BakerBooks
Grand Rapids, Michigan

Published by Baker Books
a division of Baker Publishing Group
P.O. Box 6287, Grand Rapids, MI 49516-6287
www.bakerbooks.com

Printed in the United States of America

Library of Congress Cataloging-in-Publication Data
O'Brien, Randall.
    Set free by forgiveness : the way to peace and healing / Randall O'Brien.
        p.   cm.
    Includes bibliographical references.
    ISBN 0-8010-6534-8 (pbk.)
    1. Forgiveness of sin.   I. Title.
BT795.O27   2005
241'.4—dc22   2005000970

To any I have wronged through the years;
To any who may have wronged me;
I ask your forgiveness, and give mine.
And to God, who forgives us all.

Contents

Preface

As long as I can remember I have been drawn to the topic of forgiveness. Maybe that's because I have always so badly needed to be forgiven.

One of life's greatest blessings for me personally is God's gift of my mother who instilled in her children a strong sense of right and wrong. This means, of course, that my unacceptable childhood attitudes and actions were either repressed or punished. Honesty compels me to confess that I suffered my share of punishment.

Some of my earliest memories involve prayer asking God for forgiveness. Not surprisingly, the first sermon I wrote in seminary dealt with forgiveness. Then in 1983 I heard Lewis Smedes lecture on the subject. He mesmerized me with his metaphor, insight, and relevance.

I still recall the title of Professor Smedes's lecture: "Forgiveness: What, Why, and How?" If imitation is the highest form of flattery, I have flattered Dr. Smedes since first hearing him in 1983. For over twenty years, I have taught in churches, at conferences, and on college campuses, focusing on the subject of forgiveness. Suffice it to say, I owe a great debt to Lewis Smedes. His book *Forgive and Forget: Healing*

11

the Hurts We Don't Deserve remains one of the best books available on the subject.

Owing much gratitude to many, I have gone to great pains to give credit where credit is due throughout this book. Of particular benefit to me, however, were *Dimensions of Forgiveness: Psychological Research and Theological Perspectives*, edited by Everett L. Worthington Jr.; *The Forgiving Self*, by Robert Karen; *Before Forgiving: Cautionary Views of Forgiveness in Psychotherapy*, edited by Sharon Lamb and Jeffrie G. Murphy; *Guilt and Grace*, by Paul Tournier; and Smedes's work, mentioned previously. In addition, *Forgiveness*, Issue 1 of *Christian Reflection: A Series of Faith and Ethics* (September 2001), contributed to my understanding of the issues involved in forgiveness. Much of my previously published article on forgiveness in the journal *Christian Reflection* has been reprinted here with permission. The *Forgiveness* issue and accompanying study guides are available at *www.ChristianEthics.ws*.

I would like to express my gratitude to Vicki Crumpton, Susan Fitzgerald, and Paul Brinkerhoff, my editors at Baker Books. Each labored long and hard to make this book better than otherwise it would have been. For their personal encouragement and professional expertise I am deeply appreciative.

American author Frederick Buechner is surely right when he claims, "Most theology, like most fiction, is essentially autobiography." Admittedly much of what the reader finds in this book flows from, or supports, "The Gospel According to Randall." On the other hand I must agree with my good friend Hulitt Gloer, Professor of Preaching and Christian Scriptures at the Truett Theological Seminary, and confess, "I have preached more Gospel than I have lived."

Most of us painfully realize the difference between "The Ideal Self" and "The Real Self." None of us has arrived. So how do we journey from where we are to where we want to be? In one area of life, in the realm of forgiveness, I hope this book provides a road map. If so, we will need to journey together for we are all pilgrims on the way to forgiveness.

Robert Fulghum wrote *Everything I Needed to Know I Learned in Kindergarten*. Perhaps I should write *Everything I Needed to Know about Forgiveness I Learned in My Home*. Beginning with my family of origin—Donald, Irene, Sue, and Faye—then moving to my nuclear family—Kay, Alyson Elise, Shannon, and Chris—grace upon grace has been showered upon me throughout the years. The unconditional love, forgiveness, and blessing of my family continues to transform me. I am constantly astounded that they can see me at my worst, yet steadfastly believe in my best.

Though far too numerous to name, my extended family and faithful friends through the years have taught me more about love and forgiveness "outside the home" than all the books I have read. Experience really is the best teacher; and I have experienced forgiveness from many, all of whom serve as "ghostwriters" for this book.

Finally, *the* life-shaping experience of my story remains the forgiveness of my sins by God in Christ Jesus. Receiving Christ as Lord and Savior sets me free to live new life daily. My identity as husband, father, son, brother, friend, teacher, preacher, author, disciple, neighbor, and citizen is *informed and transformed* by Christ, who reveals perfectly who God is and who we are created to be. *Love and forgiveness is what God is up to in this world*, and I want to be a part of it.

Wherever love and forgiveness bring healing, God is present, smiling, blessing the miracle of new life. Ever changing the bitter water of resentment into the sweet wine of forgiveness, God invites us all to the party. We will want to get there as soon as we can.

Randall O'Brien
Waco, Texas
January 2004

Introduction

Chris Carrier, a ten-year-old fifth grader, stepped off a school bus at approximately 1:35 p.m. on Friday, December 20, 1974, to begin his Christmas holidays. Met in his driveway by a man who claimed to be a family friend, Chris was soon driven away in a motor home, his cruel fate underway. Stopping outside of town in a lonely area the man stabbed Chris repeatedly with an ice pick. After burning Chris with lit cigarettes, the man carried Chris deep into the woods where he shot him in the head, leaving the child for dead.

The bullet entered Chris's left temple, severing his left optic nerve, and then exited through his forehead. For six days the boy lay unconscious, exposed to the elements and wild animals. Meanwhile, Chris's family grieved, prayed, posted a reward, and waited.

Christmas came. And went. No Chris. Then on December 26, the boy awoke from his coma, wandered to a nearby road, and sat by the roadside dazed until a deer hunter spotted him. Though blinded permanently in his left eye, Chris lived.

Despite lacking sufficient evidence to prosecute the case, family and law enforcement officers believed the crime was committed by David McAllister, a former employee of the family who had been fired. Charges were never brought against McAllister.

Twenty-two years later, a police officer who had been involved in the investigation discovered that David McAllister, now aged and blind from glaucoma, lay bedridden in a local nursing home. The officer went to visit McAllister. He explained to McAllister that the statute of limitations had expired in Chris's case and offered McAllister the opportunity to confess in order to find a measure of personal peace and provide Chris's family with a sense of closure in the case. McAllister readily confessed.

Chris, now thirty-two, married, with two young daughters, received a call from the officer. Over the next six days, Chris visited McAllister five times, often taking his daughters with him. "I told him that I forgave him and all there was between us now was a newfound friendship. I also told him that I had a relationship with Jesus Christ and that I wanted our friendship to extend beyond this life," Chris related.

McAllister, receiving Chris's forgiveness as well as God's, accepted Christ as his Savior. Three weeks later McAllister died. Forgiven by God and forgiven by Chris, David McAllister slept in peace.[1]

Experiences such as the Carrier-McAllister incident are hard for us to understand. *Why* would anyone commit a crime so heinous? *How* could anyone forgive an evil so great? How did Chris so freely forgive his demented attacker? When we ask someone to forgive, what is it we are asking them to do? *What* precisely is this bizarre thing called forgiveness? Besides, why *should* we forgive? *How* does one forgive even if he wants to? How would I? How *could* I?

Is forgiveness difficult for you? It is for me. I suspect forgiveness is difficult for most of us. We hurt others. We are hurt *by* others. We need to be forgiven. We need *to* forgive.

Why is pardon so unbearable to pronounce? "I forgive you for the pain you have caused me." Why is grace so awkward to request? "I want you to forgive me for hurting you."

For most of us, forgiveness isn't easy. Neither seeking nor granting pardon seems natural. Yet if we are to enjoy lives of harmony, peace, and joy, forgiveness alone provides the way. The ugly option is enslavement to a painful past.

Having a heart for forgiveness is not the best way to enjoy life; it is the only way. Nothing else works. Please consider this book an invitation to *discover the way to peace and healing, an invitation to be set free by forgiveness.*

Understanding Our Dark Side

Grab a pen and some paper. Now take a minute to describe the kind of person you despise. List the character flaws or personality traits that truly disgust you. Go ahead. Take your time. I'll wait.

Examine your list closely. Whether you want to admit it or not, you are gazing into a mirror. You have just recorded in black and white your "shadow self." By "shadow self," I mean your dark side. In reality your list reveals the person you fear you are, and the person you know you could easily become. Consequently you loathe the characteristics you wrote. Yours is a fierce struggle to repress the monster within, the dark you, reflected clearly in the light of your own handwriting. The German novelist Herman Hesse (1877–1962) wrote, "If you hate a person, you hate something in him that is part of yourself. What isn't part of ourselves doesn't disturb us."

Each of us has a dark side; each of us possesses a "shadow self." Ours is a fallen sin nature. Although the Creator created us good, our God-given freedom allows us to make moral choices. The biblical account of creation and the subsequent fall of humanity recorded in Genesis 1–3 reveal how a good creation goes bad. When the first humans chose to rebel against God, sin infected the human race. This headlong plunge into sin, known as the fall of man, was a tragedy which resulted in a fallen world where darkness and light carry on the battle for our souls to this day.

Carl Jung, a pioneer of modern psychiatry, is widely recognized for his work in the area of our dark side. In *The Archetypes and the Collective Unconscious*, Jung suggests that the shadow is the dark side of every human personality. The shadow is that part of our person which we refuse to acknowledge. Yet it is in our shadow self that we meet ourselves. An invitation is offered by our shadow self beckoning us to come to know the truth which lies within our depths.[1] British psychologist Anthony Stevens, author of *Archetype: A Natural History of the Self*, suggests we may call the shadow self our "animal nature" or the "beast within." Aspects of this animal nature include sexual lust, lust for power, and lust for aggression and destruction. Our shadow consists of the standards of behavior rejected by the immediate culture that shaped us. For instance, if profanity, sexual lusts and promiscuity, and drinking alcohol were strongly condemned in our home, extended family, church, or circle of friends, we naturally choose to repress those desires.[2] Psychologists point out that, paradoxically, the more rigid and morally legalistic our nurturing environment was, the stronger our dark side is, or the greater the temptation is for us to succumb to those very behaviors our culture rejected. Consequently we seek to repress these desires all the more, often refusing even to admit these dark desires exist.

Long before the advent of modern psychology, the apostle Paul wrote of the different sides or components of our human makeup. By employing contrasting images, he reflected accurately the conflicting polarities of our existence: flesh/spirit,

sin/righteousness, darkness/light, hatred/love, lies/truth, evil/
good, bondage/liberation, death/life.

Paul was clearly struggling with his shadow when he
penned his letter to the Romans:

> For we know that the Law is spiritual, but I am of flesh, sold into
> bondage to sin. For what I am doing, I do not understand; for I am
> not practicing what I would like to do, but I am doing the very
> thing I hate. . . . For the good that I want, I do not do, but I practice
> the very evil that I do not want. . . . I find then the principle that
> evil is present in me, the one who wants to do good.
>
> Romans 7:14–15, 19, 21

Paul's honest confession of his dark side differs from the
approach most of us follow. We prefer to live behind masks.
We labor to deceive ourselves and others. Among our many
psychological tricks we use to hide our dark side are:

projection, when we project onto others what we despise
in ourselves;

repression, when we push down beneath the surface
powerful instincts that want to come out in our lives;

denial, when we refuse to admit and face our dark side;

rationalization, when we concoct bad reasons for our bad
behavior; and

reaction-formation, when we outwardly attempt to display
the opposite of what we repress.

To varying degrees, we all are haunted by shadows within.
Paul was. I am. You are. We all are. Think about it. In our
upbringing, undesirable traits were denounced, forcing them
into our unconscious being, where they remain repressed,
but alive and dangerous. Even though we may be Christians
now, before becoming Christians, we routinely experienced
sin and darkness as we gave in to the temptations of the dark

side. Guilt and shame were present. In asking Christ to save us from our sins, we were mercifully called "out of darkness into His marvelous light" (1 Pet. 2:9). Christ is light (John 1). In him we move into the light. No one other than Christ, however, is 100 percent light (1 John 1:5). Within the rest of us, shadows exist. Even among Christians the capacity to sin remains. Temptations of the flesh force a struggle upon us. As Paul lamented, "The good that I wish, I do not do, but I practice the very evil that I do not wish" (Rom. 7:19).

Darkness and Light

As the apostle Paul acknowledged, we Christians are both flesh and spirit. By flesh here, Paul means sinful tendencies which may or may not be rebuffed in the believer's life. Jesus came in the likeness of sinful flesh (Rom. 8:3), yet he did not sin. Paul does not intend to say that flesh is evil, but that what dwells in flesh is evil, that is, sin. Since God created flesh, flesh is good.

Unredeemed persons live "according to the flesh" and are ruled by sinful desires, however. Christians too may succumb to fleshly temptations and sin (1 Cor. 3:1–3; 1 John 1:8–10). No temptation to sin comes by the Spirit. By Spirit Paul means the Spirit of God. He writes, "To set the mind on the flesh is death, but to set the mind on the Spirit is life and peace" (Rom. 8:6 NRSV). Therefore the essential distinction between life lived in "the flesh" as opposed to life in "the Spirit" lies in the absence of God's Spirit versus the ruling presence of God's Spirit in the life of the individual.

Only Christ and Satan have no shadow. One is all light; the other all darkness. The rest of us know what we need not be told: the shadow of darkness lurks within us. We have the capacity for both good and evil.

Darkness, in its perfect state, represents an absence of light. Light, in its perfect state, represents an absence of darkness.

Thus a shadow is a space sheltered from the light. Light is present as well as darkness. Welcome to the reality of our humanness! Paul testified to the presence of his shadow when he proclaimed, "I find then the principle that evil is present in me, the one who wants to do good" (Rom. 7:21). John agreed when he wrote, "If we say we have no sin, we are deceiving ourselves and the truth is not in us" (1 John 1:8). We go to great lengths to refuse to face our dark side because we do not want to suffer the guilt of acknowledging its power over us. However, to paraphrase the New Testament, without suffering, there is no salvation. Without guilt, there is no grace. Without confession, there is no cleansing. Without a crucifixion, there is no resurrection.

According to psychologists, within each of us lies a "pleasure principle" and a "reality principle." Freud called these the "Id" and the "Ego," respectively. The Id says, "I want to do the wild thing." The Ego says, "Don't be a fool. You can't do that!" One says, "Yes," the other says, "No." The pleasure principle and the reality principle constantly battle for control of our person. Ironically, the atheist Freud and the believer the apostle Paul wrote about the same inner truth.

In the Greek myth about Hercules, a time comes when Hercules must decide whether he will use his gifts for good or for evil. He leaves the Shepherds and sits alone to ponder the course his life will take. As he sits musing, two tall women approach him. One is beautiful, noble, and mod-

> *Without suffering, there is no salvation.*
> *Without guilt, there is no grace.*
> *Without confession, there is no cleansing.*
> *Without a crucifixion, there is no resurrection.*

est. The other is seductive, full-bosomed, and arrogant. The first represents virtue; the second, pleasure. Each promises

Hercules certain rewards if he chooses to follow her. The hero stands at a crossroads. Great story! Poor disguise. The *reader* is Hercules! We are *all* so tempted, aren't we? We are *one* choice away from tossing away virtue and embracing pleasure. Flesh beckons. Whether in a Greek myth or the Bible, with Hercules or with Paul, we look into the mirror, and we see ourselves.

We journey toward wholeness *not* simply by focusing on goodness, but by acknowledging, even owning, our badness. Without recognizing our dark side, we will never be authentic or complete. We must stop denying the truth we know. In his book *Make Friends with Your Shadow*, William Miller notes, "The paradox is simply that that which contains the potential for the greatest evil is at the same time *necessary* for attainment of the highest good, namely wholeness."[3] As Jung put it, "One does not become enlightened by imagining figures of light, but by making the darkness conscious."[4] The call to wholeness is a summons to trust truth, to reject deceit, to embrace the reality of our dark side.

The Power of Our Dark Side

Paul understood the power of our dark side when he confessed, "I am not practicing what I would like to do, but I am doing the very thing I hate.... but I see a different law ... waging war against the law of my mind and making me a prisoner of the law of sin ..." (Rom. 7:15, 23). Psychoanalysis teaches us that the two basic human instincts are sexual drive and aggression. Freud observed that we suppress these basic drives in order to have civilization. Otherwise we are merely barbarians. These suppressed desires constitute two powerful aspects of the shadow of every human. In the Bible and in myth, the shadow bears such names as flesh, sin, Satan, monster, dragon, serpent, darkness, and evil. Sometimes the darkness is depicted as an external threat; sometimes the danger lies within; often the peril strikes with force in a deadly combination of external and internal temptation.

In the biblical book of Revelation, the serpent, the devil, the dragon, and Satan are one (Rev. 12:9). In the mythology and folklore of almost every culture in the world, the

> *Alas, we too must face the dragons of evil, flesh, sexual lust, destructive power, and other forms of life-destroying chaos.*

dragon plays a major role as an imaginary evil beast. Dragons represent chaos and evil, and dark waters symbolize the unformed, chaotic, unconscious part of the individual. Many mythological heroes were dragon slayers: Marduk, Hercules, Apollo, Beowulf, and King Arthur, just to name a few. In the book of the Revelation given to John, Christ conquers the dragon. Alas, we too must face the dragons of evil, flesh, sexual lust, destructive power, and other forms of life-destroying chaos. We must daily slay or be slain by the powerful serpent that lurks and threatens our very being as well as creation itself.

Robert Louis Stevenson reminds us in his strangely universal and haunting story *Dr. Jekyll and Mr. Hyde* that we must not become so intrigued with the shadow that we fall under its spell. In the tale, Dr. Jekyll is a physician of upstanding character, well thought of in his community, a kind man. In his youth, Dr. Jekyll flirted with his dark side but suppressed such notions in his adult life. In experimenting with drugs, he found one that would turn his inner evil nature into an externally repulsive form. Again and again Dr. Jekyll turned himself into Mr. Hyde, his alter ego, until at last Mr. Hyde murdered a man and eventually committed suicide. Thus endeth the experiment and thus endeth

Dr. Jekyll. The story of Dr. Jekyll and Mr. Hyde warns us against playing with evil.

Doesn't Mary Shelley's horror story of Frankenstein teach us the same lesson? Dare we cultivate our dark side? Dare we dance with the devil? Could not any one of us become Frankenstein's soulless monster? Doesn't the story intend to leave us with precisely that question? Could I not become Hugh Hefner? Mae West? David the adulterer? Or Rahab the harlot? Could I not become Cain the murderer, Dr. Jekyll, or Judas Iscariot? The shadow lurks. Scripture warns, "Be of sober spirit, be on the alert. Your adversary, the devil, prowls around like a roaring lion, seeking someone to devour" (1 Peter 5:8).

Should Dr. Jekyll have fed his Mr. Hyde tendencies? What do we learn? By playing with fire, Mr. Frankenstein gave birth to a monster. Should King David have spent time alone with another man's wife? How should we respond when a snake whispers in the garden? In recent years a U.S. senator listened to his shadow, traded stamps for cash, and created a congressional postal scandal. A Wall Street high roller obeyed the whisper of the shadow, traded on insider information, and went to prison. A televangelist sowed the seeds of sexual lust and reaped a whirlwind of shame. A fellow TV preacher publicly condemned his colleague's sexual sin, calling him "a cancer on the body of Christ," then privately succumbed to the call of the wild himself, played with prostitutes, and suffered international humiliation. A Supreme Court nominee said yes to the lure of a cheap thrill and lost a seat on the bench due to skeletons in his closet who smoked marijuana!

A college president danced with the devil, embezzled millions of dollars, spent most of it on prostitutes in cities throughout the land, and went to federal prison. A sitting U.S. president, a U.S. congressman, and a presidential candidate all sauntered down temptation's seductive path falling headlong into the arms of paramours, and suffered public shame. A self-proclaimed champion of morals gambled away hundreds of thousands of dollars in seductive casinos while he authored best-selling books on virtues. America's poster boy of ultra-conservative talk radio, describing himself as "your epitome of morality and virtue," repeatedly condemned drug abusers while on the air, then used his maid to procure as many as thirty thousand illegal pills to feed his drug addiction.

America's longest-serving U.S. senator, and owner of an ugly political legacy of racism, was discovered to have fathered a child at age twenty-two, by his family's sixteen-year-old black maid. In a famous speech in 1948, the senator running as a "Dixiecrat" presidential candidate declared that there were "not enough troops in the Army to force the Southern people to break down segregation and admit the Negro race into our theaters, into our swimming pools, into our homes, and into our churches." Yet years earlier this same staunch segregationist had integrated his bed, forcing himself upon a poor black teenage girl. The dark side is real. The saying rings true: There but for the grace of God go I. And you too, by the way.

Perhaps James Thurber speaks for all of us when he wrote, "We all have our flaws. Mine is being wicked." *Time* magazine's May 25, 1987, cover story read, "What Ever Happened to Ethics?" According to the article, more than one hundred officials in the American president's administration had faced allegations of questionable activities! The "sleaze factor" in politics remains a reality in this new century. Disgusting? You bet it is! Why? Because of the repulsive immorality of it all? Yes, but also because any of us could do the same things, and we know it. Their stories are *our* stories: Samson and Delilah, David and Bathsheba, Adam and Eve, Cain and Abel, Jekyll and Hyde.

In Christopher Marlowe's *Doctor Faustus*, or Goethe's *Faust*, the leading character struggles with what we might call a midlife crisis. His repressed dark side demands attention. Rather than choosing a balanced, ordered life, Faust, or Faustus, sells his soul to Mephistopheles in exchange for the acquisition of his lustful cravings. Needless to say, disaster follows. Some of us learn from Faust. Some of us do not. But sooner or later we all stand at Faust's crossroads. Flirting with the shadow only leads to what the Bible refers to as "demon possession." The lure of the flesh pulls like a spiritual black hole. Even saintly Paul cried out with desperation, "Wretched man that I am! Who will set me free from the body of this death?" (Rom. 7:24).

Achilles, the hero and supreme warrior of the Homeric myths, possessed the qualities most of us would love to embody. He was beautiful, eloquent, courageous, mighty, courteous, generous, and wise. According to Greek mythology, Achilles' mother, Thetis, sought to make her son immortal

> We cannot correct a reality that we deny.

and invulnerable. She accomplished this by dipping him in the river Styx when he was born. She successfully dipped his small body in the river with the exception of his right heel by which she held him. This one vulnerable spot was found by a poisoned arrow from the bow of Paris, and alas Achilles died prior to the fall of Troy.

We all have an Achilles' heel, don't we? Each of us has a point of weakness, a potentially deadly area of vulnerability. After all, we are all mortal. Oftentimes we are not conscious of our weaknesses threatening to destroy us until it is too late. Other times we are all too conscious of our danger zones but refuse to acknowledge them. Meanwhile, Paris's poisoned arrow is positioned, aimed, and in flight before we can respond.

In psychological circles, a couple of axioms warn us: (1) *What we resist, persists*; and (2) *We cannot correct a reality that we deny.* Samson is the Achilles of the Bible. A mighty man of valor, Samson was the supreme warrior. For all his physical strength, however, his weakness in the sexual area of his life brought about his demise. Both Achilles and Samson had passions out of control. For Achilles, his hair-trigger rage and sensitivity to insults led to one too many fights. For Samson, his sexual lust led to one too many bedrooms. Consequently both men died tragic deaths.

Unlike Achilles and Samson, Rahab the harlot and Mary Magdalene (two famous women of the Bible) faced the reality of their dark sides. Wisely, they chose growth over grave. They elected to turn their weaknesses into growth edges. With God's help, both became renowned heroines in the kingdom of God. Rahab gave up a life of prostitution, married honorably, and was rewarded in becoming a grandmother in the line of Jesus. Mary had seven demons cast out, became one of Jesus's closest friends, and was honored with being the first person to whom Jesus appeared after his resurrection.

James and John, two of Jesus's disciples, were called "Boanerges," which means "sons of thunder." Evidently the two brothers had somewhat tumultuous personalities. Once as Jesus, James, and John traveled through a Samaritan village on their way to Jerusalem, John decided that the people of the village had failed to give Jesus the appropriate respect. Reacting angrily, John demanded, "Lord, do you want us to command fire to come down from heaven and consume

> *Every sinner has a future; every saint has a past.*

them?" (Luke 9:54 NRSV). This volatile "son of thunder" is the same John who later became affectionately known as the apostle of love, penning the following words toward the end of his life: "Beloved, let us love one another, for love is from God" (1 John 4:7).

Every sinner has a future; every saint has a past. Although Simon, another of Jesus's disciples, appeared far less than perfect in biblical passages that depict him as proud, boastful, and impetuous, his story didn't end there. In fact, his story didn't even begin there. It is true that during the events surrounding the arrest of Jesus, Simon angrily cut off a man's ear. It is also true that he used profanity. Even more heinous, it is true that Simon disloyally denied being a friend and follower of Jesus to protect himself. However, when Jesus first saw Simon, he said, "So you are Simon, the son of John? You shall be called Cephas (which means Peter)" (John 1:42 RSV). Cephas and Peter are names meaning "rock" in Aramaic and Greek, respectively. Even though Jesus knew about Simon's dark side, he saw Simon's potential to be a rock in the kingdom of God. The German poet Johann Wolfgang von Goethe explained, "Treat a man as he is and he will remain as he is. Treat a man as he can and should be and he will become as he can and should be."[5] Let it be noted: Each of us is two persons. We are the person we are. And we are the person we can become.

2

Understanding Being Sinned Against

Anyone who has read even some of the Bible can recall ample Scripture detailing our sinfulness. "There is none righteous, no, not one" (Rom. 3:10 KJV). "All have sinned and fall short of the glory of God" (Rom. 3:23). "The wages of sin is death" (Rom. 6:23). And, "All our righteousnesses are as filthy rags" (Isa. 64:6 KJV).

From church programs such as Vacation Bible School to adult Sunday school, from annual revival sermons to our pastor's weekly sermon, we have routinely heard how sinful we are. How fallen we are indeed! What sinners we are! Of course, as we know all too well, the message rings true. We are utterly selfish, sometimes cruel, often false, and generally indifferent to God and others, unless of course, it benefits us to be otherwise.

Sins Against Us

The sad fact is, we are all sinners. But we have all also been sinned against. Sins against us play a major role in shaping each one of us.

Like coming in during the middle of a movie, we often don't understand others because we don't know the events and experiences that shaped their lives. Consider the fol-

> *The sad fact is, we are all sinners.*
> *But we have all also been sinned against.*

lowing account and how the events described might have influenced this individual's life.

When my mother was pregnant with me, she told me later, a party of hooded Ku Klux Klan riders galloped up to our home in Omaha, Nebraska, one night. Surrounding the house, brandishing their shotguns and rifles, they shouted for my father to come out. . . . shouting threats, the Klansmen finally spurred their horses and galloped around the house, shattering every window pane with gun butts. Then they rode off into the night, their torches flaring . . . .

We went next, for some reason, to Lansing, Michigan, . . . my earliest vivid memory. I remember being suddenly snatched awake into a frightening confusion of pistol shots and shouting and smoke and flames. . . . Our home was burning down around us. We were lunging and bumping and tumbling all over each other trying to escape. My mother, with the baby in her arms, just made it into the yard before the house crashed in, showering sparks. I remember we were outside in the night in our underwear, crying and yelling our heads off. The white police and firemen came and stood around watching as the house burned down to the ground.

The story continues,

I remember waking up to the sound of my mother's screaming again. When I scrambled out, I saw the police in the living room; they were trying to calm her down. She had snatched on her clothes to go with them. And all of us children who were staring knew without anyone having to say it that something terrible had happened to our father.

So there we were. My mother was thirty-four years old now, with no husband, no provider or protector to take care of her eight children.[1]

Whose story is this? Malcolm X. Born an innocent baby like the rest of us, Malcolm Little was horribly sinned against. He eventually rejected his "Christian name" and assumed the name Malcolm X, dreaded leader of the Black Muslims, who described himself as "the angriest black man in America." Symbolizing hatred and violence among American blacks during the '60s, Malcolm saw whites as devils. Is it any wonder?

Whites saw Malcolm X as sinner, rather than sinned against. Don't feelings of regret, pity, repentance, shame, and compassion pull at our hearts when we know the whole

> Whites saw Malcolm X as sinner,
> rather than sinned against.

story? Doesn't fear, judgment, and hatred get crowded out by understanding? Would we have turned out any differently than Malcolm had we been wronged and wounded as he was? Who knows?

The Wounded

Not only are we willful violators of God's laws, but we are also the violated. Granted, we hurt, and we wound. But we also *are* the hurt and the wounded. All are needy. God loves us all and understands.

Each of us brings to each moment our own sad experiences. How does your childhood haunt you? Were you neglected by your father or rejected by your mother? Was a sibling favored over you? Were you abused emotionally, verbally, physically, or sexually? Did the cruel taunts of other children target you? Did you find others to be better than you in those things that mattered most, leaving you suffering from low self-esteem, as others mocked you, and left you out of the fun? How did poverty or wealth distort your view of yourself?

Childhood memories may warm and inspire us. For that we are grateful. Be that as it may, insecurity, prejudice, fears, low self-image, and various and sundry complexes often result from our having been sinned against in childhood. We all have been oppressed and wounded. Our point of woundedness is where grace comes in. Grace understands that we are all precious children of God, created in God's image. In our ministry to each other, let us not lose sight of those who have been sinned against. Insight into another's experience can steer us toward love, understanding, pity,

> God calls us to do three things:
> to come, become, and overcome.

compassion, acceptance, and grace, rather than scorn, self-righteousness, and condemnation. Clearly God wishes all to come to his banquet table. Grace is our meal ticket.

Jesus was sinned against, yet he never became a sinner. The goal of understanding another's experience is not to remove responsibility, but to supply grace. Each of us is responsible for our choices, and each of us needs grace. We are Christians, not libertines. Libertines would claim, "We are at liberty to do as we please." Jesus Christ says, in essence, "I love you and understand why you do what you do. Bad things also happened to me. But let us see all things as opportunities for personal spiritual growth and occasions for displaying the love of God. I died that you might be well. I love you. Be healed. Follow me."

We all sin and we are all sinned against. Grace, understanding, and forgiveness flow from heaven and from God's people. Please don't misunderstand, no one's sin is excused. Rather, our sins are forgiven. God doesn't give anyone permission to be a scoundrel. On the contrary, God calls us to do three things: to *come*, *become*, and *overcome*. We *come* to God, to *become* who we are created to be, and to *overcome* obstacles along the way. Our model is Christ. Our goal is Christlikeness.

The writer of the letter to the Hebrews encourages us in this way:

> Let us also lay aside every encumbrance and the sin which so easily entangles us, and let us run with endurance the race that is set before us, fixing our eyes on Jesus, the author and perfecter of faith, who for the joy set before Him endured the cross, despising the shame, and has sat down at the right hand of the throne of God. For consider Him who has endured such hostility by sinners against Himself, so that you will not grow weary and lose heart. . . . Therefore, strengthen the hands that are weak and the knees that are feeble, and make straight paths for your feet, so that the limb which is lame may not be put out of joint, but rather be healed.
>
> Pursue peace with all men, and the sanctification without which no one will see the Lord. See to it that no one comes short of the grace of God; that no root of bitterness springing up causes trouble, and by it many be defiled.
>
> Hebrews 12:1–3, 12–15

Things that happen *to* us often fall outside our control. However, what happens *in* us and *through* us awaits our decision.

My mother was a beautiful woman, dark, mixed Indian and Negro. I found out early in my childhood what happened to her. When I was a baby she was raped and murdered by three white men one night. Before my father went to look for her, he took me to his best friend's house and said, "Keep her until I come back." My father never came back.[2]

These are the words of Daisy Bates, one of America's most famous civil rights activists of the twentieth century. Her adoptive father once told her, "Daisy, you're consumed with hatred for white people. If you're gonna hate, make it count for something. Hate segregation in the South." Daisy began a newspaper in Little Rock, Arkansas. Later, as president of the Arkansas National Association for the Advancement of Colored People (NAACP), she led a movement to desegregate the city, winning international acclaim leading the successful fight of the Little Rock Nine to desegregate Little Rock Central High School in 1957.[3]

Daisy suffered at the hands of evil. Rather than succumbing to evil's lure to remain bitter, she chose to become better by first "being healed," and then "making straight paths" for countless feet.

"Hey, kid, are you a kike?" "I don't know," the little boy answered. He had never heard the word "kike" before. Mike Gold wrote in his book *A Jew without Knowing It* that his mother had warned him not to wander beyond four streets. On this particular day, Mike had wandered too far. "Are you a Christ-killer?" "I don't know," the child responded again. "Where do you live?" the gang demanded. Mike told them.

> "Daisy, you're consumed with hatred for white people. If you're gonna hate, make it count for something. Hate segregation in the South."

"So you are a kike; you are a Christ-killer. Well you're in Christian territory, and we are Christians. We're going to teach you to stay where you belong!"

John Powell retold Mike's story in his book, *Why Am I Afraid to Love*. He related how the little boy was beaten, bloodied, and taunted as the gang sent him home. "We are Christians, and you killed Christ! Stay where you belong!" When Mike's mother saw him, she asked hysterically, "Who did this to you?" "I don't know," the frightened boy answered. As his mother held and rocked her little boy to soothe him, Mike whispered to her, "Mama, who is Christ?"[4]

The philosopher of American Communism in the 1920s was a Jew named Mike Gold, yes, this same Mike Gold. Powell relates that Gold died in 1967 taking his last meals in a Catholic charity in New York City run by Dorothy Day. Day once said of Gold: "Mike Gold eats every day at the table of Christ, but he will probably never accept him because of the day he first heard his name."[5]

Yes, it is true: We, like sheep, have all gone astray. Some into the Black Muslims; some into communism; some onto paths of hurting themselves, God, and others. Indeed, it is true.

> *Should we not breathe prayers of grace, love, and forgiveness for all?*

We are all sinners. May God help us remember, though, that we have all been sinned against as well. Henry Wadsworth Longfellow opined, "If we could read the secret history of our enemies, we should find in each man's life sorrow and suffering enough to disarm all hostility."[6] Should we not then be kind to one another? Should we not pity each other? Should we not breathe prayers of grace, love, and forgiveness for all?

3

Guilt and Shame

Everyone struggles with guilt. We all wear fig leaves and hide our apple cores. Each of us lives in exile from Eden. Every one of us yearns to return home. Many roads beckon, but alas, lead nowhere. We should follow the sign marked, "Grace." Grace is the way home.

What is guilt and what causes it? Paul Tournier distinguishes between false guilt and true guilt in his book *Guilt and Grace*. False guilt comes from the judgments of others. True guilt results from divine judgment, or the violation of the innermost values of our hearts.

Healthy guilt strikes when we: (1) say or do something wrong, (2) consider saying or doing something wrong, (3) fail to say or do something we feel is right to say or do, or (4) consider not saying or doing the right thing. Guilt, erupting from sources other than these four, is unhealthy and begs professional attention. (False guilt, or unhealthy guilt, may be traced to childhood where a low self-image

39

originates in relation to parents and significant others.) Healthy guilt, or true guilt, springs from the violation of an accepted standard. The purposes of healthy guilt are:

> *Everyone struggles with guilt. We all wear fig leaves and hide our apple cores. Each of us lives in exile from Eden. Every one of us yearns to return home.*

(1) to serve as a warning, and (2) to motivate us. This warning serves notice that we are going against the value system instilled within us, and it motivates us to amend our thoughts and behavior.

Michael Lewis distinguishes between guilt and shame in his book *Shame: The Exposed Self.* According to Lewis, shame is broad; guilt is specific. Shame says, "I am a bad person." Guilt says, "What I did was bad." Like guilt, shame visits each human heart. Shame makes us want to hide, to escape from the piercing eyes of others, to disappear. Adam and Eve provide an obvious example of individuals afflicted with shame. They sin, realize they are naked, seek to cover their shame with fig leaves, then finally attempt to hide from God. When we violate a moral standard, shame finds us. We feel we are no good. The self focuses upon the self and pronounces judgment: "Unworthy!"

Guilt inevitably produces fear. What we fear is punishment. Adam and Eve hid because they feared punishment from God. Cain feared retribution from others because he murdered his brother. Guilt may be resolved or unresolved. Left

> *How we choose to respond to guilt makes all the difference.*

unresolved, guilt leads to hardness of heart, mean-spiritedness, aggression, anger, fear, and anxiety. Resolved guilt, on the other hand, leads to relief, assurance of pardon, relaxation, joy, peace, and security. How we choose to respond to guilt makes all the difference.

Responding to Our Guilt

We have two basic choices when we recognize our guilt: denial or confession. The biblical recommendation is clear enough when we compare the following passages: "Behold, I will enter into judgment with you because you say, 'I have not sinned'" (Jer. 2:35). Then, "If we say that we have no sin, we are deceiving ourselves and the truth is not in us. If we confess our sins, He is faithful and righteous to forgive us our sins and to cleanse us from all unrighteousness. If we say that we have not sinned, we make Him a liar and His word is not in us" (1 John 1:8–10).

Old Testament Examples

In the Old Testament, Israelite kings Saul and David illustrate respectively the wrong way and the right way to handle guilt. The Philistines assembled to fight the Israelites, bringing thirty thousand chariots, six thousand horsemen, and warriors as numerous as the sand on the seashore. Saul waited in vain for Samuel, the prophet and priest, to arrive to offer a sacrifice to God so he would be prepared for the inevitable battle. Being impatient, Saul took it upon himself to offer a burnt offering to the Lord, a practice reserved for priests only. When Samuel eventually arrived, he asked, "What have you done?" (For a king to usurp priestly duties by leading in religious ritual was forbidden.) Saul replied, "Because I saw that the people were scattering from me, and that you did not come within the appointed days, and that the Philistines were assembling at Michmash, . . . I forced myself and offered the burnt offering" (1 Sam. 13:11–12).

Regrettably, Saul chose to ignore or repress his conscience, to justify his actions, and to blame others for his folly. The people, Samuel, and the Philistines were all to blame, not Saul. King Saul refused to take responsibility for his action. "You have acted foolishly," Samuel announced to Saul.

At a later date, Samuel commanded Saul, saying, "Thus says the LORD of hosts, . . . go and strike Amalek and utterly destroy all that he has, and do not spare him; but put to death both man and woman, child and infant, ox and sheep, camel and donkey" (1 Sam. 15:3). Saul indeed defeated the Amalekites. "But Saul and the people spared

> King Saul illustrates the wrong way to handle guilt. Ignoring our conscience, justifying our actions, or blaming others for our wrongdoing are all responses to guilt which lead to self-destruction.

Agag and the best of the sheep, the oxen, the fatlings, the lambs, and all that was good, and were not willing to destroy them utterly; but everything despised and worthless, that they utterly destroyed" (1 Sam. 15:9). Once again, the prophet confronted the king about his disobedience. Saul, however, declared, "Blessed are you of the LORD! I have carried out the command of the LORD." Samuel responded, "What then is this bleating of the sheep in my ears, and the lowing of the oxen which I hear?" (1 Sam. 15:13–14).

Uh-oh. Saul first disobeyed God, then misrepresented the truth, and finally was caught red-handed. His response. "The people took some of the spoil, sheep and oxen . . ." (1 Sam. 15:21). Unrepentant, Saul again turned to his blamer personality. Therefore the prophet pronounced God's judgment upon the king. "Rebellion is as the sin of divination, and insubordination is as iniquity and idolatry. Because you have rejected the word of the LORD, He has also rejected you from being king" (1 Sam. 15:23). Thus Saul's eventual loss of the throne was self-inflicted.

King Saul illustrates the wrong way to handle guilt. Ignoring our conscience, justifying our actions, or blaming others for our wrongdoing are all responses to guilt which lead to self-destruction. The first couple is another example of individuals who modeled an ill-advised pattern of response to guilt and shame in the Garden. Adam blamed Eve, and maybe even God ("The woman whom You gave to be with me, she gave me from the tree, and I ate" [Gen. 3:12]); Eve blamed the serpent. Saul was not the first, nor will he be the last, to try to hide behind a blamer personality when confronted with his guilt.

Like Saul, as with each of us, David asserted his own will over God's, thereby sinning. In one of the best-known stories in the Bible, David committed adultery with Bathsheba (2 Samuel 11). One spring during a time of war, King David sent his army off to battle. He, however, remained behind. One evening David arose from his couch to enjoy a stroll on the roof of his palace. From his elevated walkway, he saw a beautiful woman bathing. Toying with temptation, he dispatched a servant to discover her identity. Despite being married himself, despite learning that Bathsheba was the wife of Uriah (one of his soldiers), and despite his covenant to keep the Ten Commandments, which include a prohibition against adultery, David sent for Bathsheba and slept with her. When she became pregnant, David brought Uriah in from the battlefield under the pretense of desiring a report on the troops. David's solution to his dilemma was to have Uriah sleep with Bathsheba before returning to camp in order to provide cover for the king's sin. Uriah, however, refused each opportunity to be with his wife on consecutive nights, declining the privilege of being comfortable while his fellow soldiers slept in tents. David ultimately designed a successful plot for Uriah's death in battle and married Bathsheba, assuming his cover-up had achieved its purpose. Not so.

God sent Nathan the prophet to confront David and hopefully convict him of his sins of adultery and murder. The prophet of God told a tale, cleverly devised to impli-

> David's response to his guilt differs radically from Saul's. David's is the right way to handle guilt: He accepted responsibility for his actions; he recognized and confessed his guilt; he repented; and he received God's forgiveness.

cate David by appealing to his sense of justice. Playing the part of righteous ruler, David unwittingly passed judgment upon himself. "Guilty!" cried David, of the wicked character in the prophet's story. "You are the man!" declared the prophet.

How did David respond to his guilt? Not in the wrong way. Not by seeking to repress his conscience; not by justifying his behavior; and not by blaming others. "I have sinned against the LORD," David confessed (2 Sam. 12:13).

The superscription attached to Psalm 51 designates the hymn as "a Psalm of David, when Nathan the prophet came to him, after he had gone in to Bathsheba." According to the psalm, David prayed,

> Be gracious to me, O God, according to Your lovingkindness . . .
> Wash me thoroughly from my iniquity
>   and cleanse me from my sin.
> For I know my transgressions,
>   and my sin is ever before me.

Against You, You only, I have sinned
   and done what is evil in Your sight,
so that You are justified when You speak
   and blameless when You judge.

Psalm 51:1–4

David's response to his guilt differs radically from Saul's. David's is the right way to handle guilt: He accepted responsibility for his actions; he recognized and confessed his guilt; he repented; and he received God's forgiveness. Consequently Nathan announced, "The LORD also has taken away your sin; you shall not die" (2 Sam. 12:13).

David prayed for renewal, begging, "Create in me a clean heart, O God, and renew a steadfast spirit within me. Do not cast me away from Your presence and do not take Your Holy Spirit from me" (Ps. 51:10–11). Groaning in hope, David prayed, "A broken and a contrite heart, O God, You will not despise" (Ps. 51:17). David's hope was no longer in deceit, but in the Deity.

There is a right way and a wrong way to handle our guilt. In broad terms, denial is wrong; confession is right. Denial leads to hell; confession leads to heaven, here and now, and in the life to come. The difference in the destinies of Saul and David may be traced to the manner in which each responded to his guilt. David accepted his blame; Saul did not. Saul was rejected as king by God; David was chosen as king by God to replace Saul.

New Testament Examples

In New Testament times, the Pharisees were acutely in tune with sin and guilt. Rather than accepting their own sinfulness, however, they found it easier to project it onto others. So they took to the streets looking for evil easier to face than their own. Finding a woman to accuse of adultery, they managed to employ a mechanism of deflection, conveniently diverting attention, theirs and others, away from their own iniquities. This slick move is called "projection," since we project our badness onto others. Jesus was not fooled and said, "He who is without sin among you, let him be the first to throw a stone at her" (John 8:7).

Among Jesus's disciples, guilt tortured both Judas and Simon Peter. Judas, unable to resolve his guilt for betraying Jesus, eventually committed suicide. Peter's guilt came from denying Jesus three times on the eve of his Lord's crucifixion, leaving Peter to live with his shame.

After his death and burial, the resurrected Jesus came and stood among his disciples, saying, "Peace be with you." Peter saw him and heard him, but something remained unresolved between Peter and Jesus. Some time afterward, perhaps not knowing what else to do, Peter announced, "I am going fishing." That's where Jesus found him, as before, by the shore of the Sea of Galilee. Though their meeting was awkward at first, at least for Peter, Jesus's forgiveness of Peter's thrice betrayal soon flooded his soul. Peter's guilt melted before his Lord's grace. The "Rock," which Jesus had foreseen in Simon from the start, became a reality in the years ahead as the forgiven disciple faithfully served the Lord, "feeding his sheep." The "Rock," in time, even bravely followed his Master into martyrdom.

Another marvelous picture of God's grace in the face of our guilt and shame is revealed in Jesus's parable of the prodigal son. According to the parable, a wasteful son had made a mess of his life in loose living in a country far from his family. Nonetheless his loving father longed for the boy to return home. One day the father saw his son coming in the distance. Running to meet his son, the father embraced and kissed him. Soon the father was giving gifts to his son and throwing a party with great rejoicing! All was forgiven; grace was present. Jesus told this story, in part, to show how God, our Father in heaven, longs to shower us with grace and forgiveness. Indeed, grace and forgiveness await *every* prodigal daughter and son.

Coming Home to Grace

While awaiting trial, pickax murderer Karla Faye Tucker, a prodigal daughter, "came home." Karla confessed her sins, repented, and received Christ as her Savior. "When I was forgiven and experienced forgiveness," she shared, "it freed me inside to soar. I went higher and deeper with the Lord."[1]

My good friends Mary Alice and Charlie Wise became like family to Karla. For years the Wises have led a Bible

> Grace and forgiveness await
> every prodigal daughter and son.

study on Tuesday nights in the Mountain View Prison Unit for women in Gatesville, Texas, where Karla was incarcerated on death row. Mary Alice and Charlie once told me that Karla was one of the most radiant Christians they have ever known. In Linda Storm's book *Set Free*, the author quotes Mary Alice as saying, "The thing that affects me most about Karla is the way she completely disarms people with the love of God. I have never met anyone with such all-out love for Jesus."[2]

Karla discovered the saving truth of God's grace that John proclaimed when he wrote, "My little children, I am writing these things to you so that you may not sin. And if anyone sins, we have an Advocate with the Father, Jesus Christ the righteous; and He Himself is the propitiation for our sins; and not for ours only, but also for those of the whole world" (1 John 2:1–2).

How do we get rid of our guilt and shame? First, we "own" it or confess it. Next, we remove ourselves from the source of our wrongdoing. Jesus illustrated this principle in the Sermon on the Mount when he taught,

> If your right eye makes you stumble, tear it out and throw it from you. . . . If your right hand makes you stumble, cut it off and throw it from you; for it is better for you to lose one of the parts of your body, than for your whole body to go into hell.
>
> Matthew 5:29–30

Was Jesus introducing mutilation as a spiritual discipline? Hardly! Removing an eye or a hand cannot remove the lust of the flesh within us. Jesus was saying that we should separate ourselves from whatever causes us to do wrong. We should acknowledge the problem and take drastic action to correct it.

The biblical word for correcting our sin problem is *repentance*. Repentance differs from confession. Confession acknowledges the problem; repentance does something about the problem. To repent is to turn around and go in a different direction. To repent is to turn *from* sin and turn *to* God. Since true guilt and shame result from unacceptable thoughts or behavior, or what the Bible calls "sin," our problem must be dealt with at its source.

Owning our guilt and repenting, that is, removing ourselves from the source of our wrongdoing and turning to God, are the first two steps on the road to peace and healing. But those two steps alone do not set us free. For true freedom, we need the wonderful gift of forgiveness through God's grace.

German pastor and theologian Dietrich Bonhoeffer noted correctly that the last word with Christ is grace. But you can't speak that last word until you've spoken the next-to-last word: guilty![3] Yes, it is true. We are all guilty. "For all have sinned and fall short of the glory of God" (Rom. 3:23). So we confess. We repent. Ah, but grace awaits! We are forgiven "as a gift by His grace through the redemption which is in Christ Jesus" (Rom. 3:24). Oh, happy day! Our guilt is washed away.

4

What Is Forgiveness?

God created us for togetherness. We are social beings. God's idea of a good creation calls for us his creatures to live in a love relationship with God and with each other. Simply put, we are created to love God with all our heart, soul, and might; then we are to love our neighbor as we love ourselves (Matt. 22:37–40). That is God's design for us.

Something, however, has gone terribly wrong. The universal story of humankind finds tragic expression in the saga of the first family. Enjoying the option of living in an intimate relationship with God in the Garden of Eden or breaking from the path of peace to travel their own road to rebellion, Adam and Eve chose poorly. Rather than saying yes to God, they bellowed, "No!" Choosing separateness over oneness with their Creator, they lost Eden.

Why would anyone choose the Land of Nod (wandering) over the Garden with God? Why would anyone prefer the wilderness of estrangement over a life of intimacy? Why would anyone race madly down the road toward death rather than walk serenely down the path of life?

We need not ask Adam and Eve. We need only ask ourselves. We have all chosen foolishly. Adam means "humankind." Eve means "the mother of all living ones." The story of Adam and Eve is representative of every living human being stumbling blindly in the wilderness, longing to return to Eden. The story of Adam and Eve is our story. But there is more.

Estrangement from God in the first family soon gave birth to brotherly strife, alienation, and death. The history of the children of Adam and Eve provides the sequel, the next

> *Forgiveness is the removal of personal barriers within a relationship caused by wrongdoing, real or imagined.*

gruesome portrait of ourselves. Jealous of his brother, Cain, whose name means "spear," slays Abel, whose name means "breath" or "wind," which symbolizes the fleeting nature of life. Alas, alienation turns friends into aliens. Estrangement creates strangers. Enmity begets enemies. Then what?

In just the first four chapters of the Bible we have already seen ourselves portrayed all too clearly. In short, we are doers of wrong. Rebels. We are selfish. We are, to use the biblical term, "sinners." Moreover, wrongdoing always costs us dearly whether we are the victim or the villain.

Danger lurks wherever we find animosity, resentment, and estrangement. Might forgiveness save us from the danger?

First, we need to define "forgiveness." Exactly what is forgiveness? *Forgiveness is the removal of personal barriers within a relationship caused by wrongdoing, real or imagined.* Forgiveness heals the wounds of separation and allows interpersonal healing to begin. Forgiveness is medicine for the soul. It is a miracle drug for a fatal disease.

Jimmy Lee Gray is dead now. Some say he should have been dead long ago. Others say he should still be alive. Still others say he never should have been born. But he's dead now. So are his victims.

In a fit of rage, while on a date with his teenage sweetheart, Jimmy Lee Gray seized his girlfriend by the throat and violently began to shake and strangle her until her lifeless corpse slumped quietly onto the car seat. Seven years later, free on parole from a prison in Arizona, he made his way to Mississippi where he struck again. In Pascagoula, Mississippi, he abducted an innocent three-year-old girl, carried her into a wooded area, and performed various perverted and tortuous acts upon her person. Then, seized by guilt and demonic forces, he held her precious little head under a muddy puddle of water until her helpless last kick fell silently against the water. Jimmy Lee Gray dragged her limp little body to a bridge and threw it into a dark watery grave.[1]

Dare we ask the parents of these two innocent victims to forgive Jimmy Lee Gray? How could they possibly forgive him for his barbaric crimes? For that matter, how do *we* for-

> *The biblical words most frequently used to speak of forgiveness mean "to lift up," "to bear," "to dismiss or send away."*

give someone who wrongs *us*, whether gravely or slightly? Besides, why should we forgive anyway? But suppose we somehow decide we *want* to forgive. How do we actually do it? Precisely what is forgiveness?

The biblical words most frequently used to speak of forgiveness mean "to lift up," "to bear," "to dismiss or send away." These definitions imply that something needs to be removed for forgiveness to occur. With forgiveness, sins are sent away and individuals are drawn closer together. Forgiveness rids relationships of bitter personal barriers.

God removed the barriers that Gray's crimes had erected between himself and Jimmy Lee Gray. While awaiting execution on death row in the Parchman State Penitentiary in the Mississippi Delta, Gray met Tommy Ellis, a volunteer chaplain. The two became friends. As Ellis shared Jimmy Lee's last meal with him minutes before Gray walked to the electric chair, they prayed together. Jimmy Lee asked God to forgive him. Confessing his sins, he accepted Jesus Christ as his Savior. Jimmy Lee Gray died forgiven by God.

If God can pardon sins of this magnitude and drastically smaller ones as well, surely you and I should be able to forgive each other when we snub each other or gossip about each other. Of course, not all wrongs are trivial. Regardless of the magnitude of the wrong, forgiveness is never easy.

When we stop and think about it, forgiveness is really a process and consists of four stages.

Hurt

The first stage of forgiveness may seem obvious but is important to recognize: We can only forgive when we have been *hurt*. Unless someone has harmed us in some fashion, we do not suffer a crisis of forgiveness. God had one Son who was without sin, but none of God's children escape suffering. Sooner or later we all hurt.

Authors and researchers, including Lewis Smedes, Everett Worthington Jr., Robert Karen, Sharon Lamb, and others, have written extensively about forgiveness. All agree that without hurt, forgiveness is impossible. Moreover, there are several characteristics of the kind of hurt that begs forgiveness.

In order to create a crisis of forgiveness, hurt must be *personal*. We are injured within the context of relationships.

Persons wound us. Although nature, the economy, corporations, schools, or other organizations may inflict pain or grief, for the most part our animosity focuses on individuals within these organizations. To be sure, we often nurse bitter feelings toward a school, company, store, agency, or government. Tragedy may even erupt as a result of enmity toward an institution, as it did with Timothy McVeigh in his cruel bombing of the federal building in Oklahoma City. However, open wounds result primarily from interpersonal battles, even within organizations.

In addition to being *personal*, injuries requiring forgiveness must be *unfair*. Generally, we suffer from a crisis of forgiveness when our sense of fairness is violated. If I expect to be treated justly but am treated unjustly, I am likely to experience strong feelings of resentment. Whenever we receive less than we expect or think we deserve, we feel hurt.

Hurts that are *intentional* are deeply painful and require forgiveness for healing to occur. *Unintentional* hurts are just that—unintentional. Although accidental injury may also require the hard work of forgiveness, resolution is often easy. For instance, I was once urinated and defecated upon. However, I had absolutely no impulse to forgive. The offending party—my daughter—was only six months old.

> Whenever we receive less than we expect
> or think we deserve, we feel hurt.

On October 1, 1950, the comic strip character Charlie Brown was introduced to the world in nine newspapers. The creator of the strip, Charles Schulz, later revealed that his inspiration came from an event he witnessed in seventh grade. Two of the more popular girls in his class eagerly approached the class "ugly duckling" and exclaimed, "We're going to have a party this week, and we're going to invite all the girls in the class, except you."[2]

The uninvited girl was devastated. Remembering that moment, Schulz devoted the *Peanuts* comic strip, in part, to the theme of cruelty among children. Intentional harm such as Schulz witnessed either festers or heals depending upon the victim's response to it.

Two other kinds of hurts, which damage if not destroy relationships, are *disloyalty* and *betrayal*. Barriers appear instantly when disloyalty and betrayal are present in a relationship. Your bosom buddy is not there for you in your hour of need. Your lover, your friends report, is secretly seeing someone else. Your spouse of many years leaves you and your children for "a meaningful relationship" with someone from work. Your close friend joins in the gossip of your enemies and reveals your secret shame. Betrayal stabs you like a dagger in the back. Forgiveness is essential to repair these relationships.

Yet another such hurt necessitating forgiveness is *brutality*. For instance, being made fun of humiliates us, wounds us, and throws us into an interpersonal state of emergency. You are mocked for being fat, or skinny, or short, or tall, or uncoordinated, or dumb. You feel exposed and shamed when you only want to be left alone. Taunts brutalize.

Dr. Martin Luther King Jr. knew brutality firsthand. During the civil rights movement of the '50s and '60s, he joined his voice to countless innocent voices crying out in outrage from their graves. Recalling the pain of being kicked, cursed, and beaten by vicious mobs, Dr. King boldly decried the evils of racism. Relating the anguish of watching his children develop an unconscious bitterness toward white people, he lamented the hate-filled syllables spat at him, his family, and friends. In his book *Why We Can't Wait*, Dr. King grieved,

> When you have seen vicious mobs lynch your mothers and fathers at will and drown your sisters and brothers at whim; when you have seen hate-filled policemen curse, kick and even kill your black brothers and sisters; when you see the vast majority of your twenty million Negro brothers smothering in an airtight

cage of poverty in the midst of an affluent society; when you suddenly find your tongue twisted and your speech stammering as you seek to explain to your six-year-old daughter why she can't go to the public amusement park that has just been advertised on television, and see tears welling up in her eyes when she is told that Funtown is closed to colored children, and see ominous clouds of inferiority beginning to form in her little mental sky . . . ; when you have to concoct an answer for a five-year-old son who is asking: "Daddy, why do white people treat colored people so mean?" . . . ; when you are humiliated day in and day out by nagging signs reading "white" and "colored"; when your first name becomes "nigger," your middle name becomes "boy," (however old you are) . . . and your wife and mother are never given the respected title "Mrs."; when you are forever fighting a degenerating sense of "nobodiness"—then you will understand. . . .[3]

The first stage on the road to forgiveness is *hurt*. Have you been hurt?

Alienation

The second stage on the journey to forgiveness is *alienation*. God created us to live in relational harmony with him and each other. Sin breaches relationships, causing a distressful

> *Love is the answer to the problem of alienation in human existence. Love unites.*

rift between us. Although the problem may be described in different ways—sometimes as a painful gulf, other times as isolation by barriers—the issue is always separation—*alienation*. When we are hurt, oneness is lost. The dis-ease of disunity devours the ease of unity.

In his book *The Art of Loving*, the noted psychoanalyst Eric Fromm contends that the problem of human existence is alienation, separation, and estrangement. He argues that life is one futile attempt after another to escape from the dungeon of our aloneness.[4]

Love is the answer to the problem of alienation in human existence. Love unites. When love is absent, isolation is present. We were not created to live in bitter isolation from each other. Distance diminishes us. When we wrong another person, or are wronged by another, distance results. Peace becomes the first casualty of wrongdoing. Peace implies unity, wholeness. How can we possibly live in peace when we are hurting each other? When we hurt each other, ease surrenders to dis-ease. We feel sick and alone. Heaven on Earth vanishes. Hell on Earth engulfs us. Flames of resentment rage and threaten to consume us.

In his play *No Exit*, Jean-Paul Sarte writes, "Hell is other people."[5] He did not write, "Heaven is other people," but he well might have. Indeed both claims prove true. Do we not find that the stuff of heaven or hell on earth flows from the heart of our relationships? Intimacy blesses us with heaven; isolation curses us with the opposite.

When Mrs. Lambert discovered that her new next-door neighbor Sean McGraw was a minister, she could hardly contain herself. Her husband was not a Christian. In fact, try as she might, she had never been able to ignite even a spark of interest in her husband regarding anything religious. "I just know God is going to use you," she exclaimed. "It is no accident that we have moved in next door."

More than a year passed. Then one fall afternoon as Mrs. Lambert and Reverend McGraw were each retrieving the day's mail, they met at the end of their driveways where Mrs. Lambert revealed her version of the mystery of God's plan. "I knew God brought us here for a purpose," she shared. "I just knew it. George is going to have open-heart surgery next week," she continued. "I really think this is the time God is going to use you to lead George to Christ."

It made no difference that Reverend McGraw fully intended to be of whatever help he could to the Lambert family. Nor did it matter that during Mr. Lambert's stay in the hospital, extenuating circumstances prevented the minister from making a visit. All that mattered to Mrs. Lambert was that her neighbor ended up letting her down. Her hopes trampled, Mrs. Lambert felt betrayed. Alienation built a fence between their yards. The neighbors' relationship suffered from a crisis of forgiveness.

Release

The third stage on the journey to forgiveness is *release*. Any time we are harmed by another person, an urgent choice presses against us. We can choose to hold a grudge, or we can choose to let it go. Remember the biblical definitions of forgiveness are "to send away, to dismiss, to remove." In forgiveness, obstacles blocking friendship are removed.

Some years ago I suffered the daily bruises of personal insult from a man associated with my work. Since vocation caused our paths to cross frequently, escape eluded me. Verbal arrows aimed at me hit their mark time and again. Snide remarks, degrading innuendoes, sadistic humor persisted relentlessly. Cruel words cut like razors. "Sticks and stones may break my bones, but words *hurt worst of all*." Then I learned that comments made to others about me by this same acquaintance were equally brutal. My initial response was hurt. Then anger. Eventually reason prevailed. I committed myself to trying harder to be his friend. When that failed, I was determined to be intentional about saying good things about my nemesis to all who knew us both. Of course I hoped the compliments would be passed along and change his view of me. Nice try. Next, I tried giving him a friendship gift, carefully chosen, one I knew he would like. Nothing doing. Finally, I gave up, deciding to hate the man who obviously hated me. I decided to call Possum, my shade tree counselor.

When all the world goes mad, only the mad seem sane. Of course Possum isn't really mad. Folks just say he is. They whisper, "He's been out in the sun too long." Or, "That ol' boy is one enchilada shy of a combination plate." Now I will admit, Possum talks "different." The first time I met him he asked, "Is it shorter to New York City or by bus?" Later he came to my home, rang the doorbell, and greeted me with, "Do you live here or ride a bicycle?" He mumbles things like, "I feel more like I do now than I did awhile ago." Possum is a sage.

Anyway I called my friend. "Possum, look, I need some counsel," I shared. "How 'bout if I buy you a deli sandwich and a root beer, and you listen to this mess I'm in? I could sure use some good advice right about now," I confessed. "What do ya think?"

Sitting there eating sandwiches, Possum listened to the entire story. When I finished, I said, "Possum, I think I'm 'bout ready to hate his guts!" "Now Reverend, Reverend, Reverend," he countered, "Never judge a man, Reverend, until

> "Never judge a man, Reverend, until you've walked a mile in his shoes. When you do that, you'll be a mile away from him, and he won't have any shoes!"

you've walked a mile in his shoes. When you do that, you'll be a mile away from him, and he won't have any shoes!"

Possum is a genius. When slighted we must find an alternative to the "judge and grudge" approach. Letting the slight go, trying to understand, offers a sane path to follow when insults shove us down the road toward anger.

Our challenge is to redirect the focus from ourselves as victim to consideration of the other person as being the truly needy one. Seeing the other individual as weak, pitiful, and needy grants us a perspective for ministry. Daring to leave ourselves and our misery behind in favor of reflecting on ways to alleviate the obvious inner misery of the pain-giver brings light into the darkness. We can then see clearly how best to minister.

The saying rings true, "Those who deserve love the least, need it the most." Jimmy Lee Gray needed love. Did you know that Jimmy Lee Gray's father would not even *look* at him? The boy would cut school to run to his father's construction job site, timing his arrival to coincide with his father's breaks or lunch. Why? He yearned to spend time with his

> "Those who deserve love the least, need it the most."

father. He longed to receive a touch, a word, a glance, anything from the man he loved. It never came. The other construction workers would plead, "For God's sake, Gray, look at the boy. Speak to him. Anything!" Nothing. Later, the family would not even accept Jimmy Lee's body for burial.

Given the savage butchery of blacks during the civil rights movement, we would expect Dr. King to have been bitter. However, after his murder, Mrs. King reflected, "My husband often told the children that if a man had nothing that was worth dying for, then he was not fit to live. He said also that it's not how long you live, but how well you live." Then she added, "He never hated."[6]

Dr. King's home was bombed. He was jailed in Montgomery and ultimately assassinated. Yet in his sermon entitled, "Loving Your Enemies," he cried, "To our most bitter opponents we say: . . . Do to us what you will, and we shall continue to love you. . . . Throw us in jail, and we shall still love you. Bomb our homes and threaten our children, and we shall still love you."[7]

Dr. King had given it all to God. Have you?

Reunion

The fourth and final leg of the journey to forgiveness is *reunion*. We are friends again. Brothers again. Sisters again. Neighbors again. Loved ones again. Ourselves again. Forgiveness reestablishes the freedom of friendship. Our relationship is restored, at least as far as *we* are concerned. Grudges flee out the back door as pardon walks in the front door. Hatred loses. Love wins. Victims become victors. Peace triumphs over pride. Rest rocks you to sleep at night and rage disappears. Reunion happens. At least in *your* heart, it happens.

Forgiveness happens to the person doing it. It may or may not affect the person being forgiven. Forgiveness is a one-way street. Reconciliation is a two-way street. Reconciliation results only when forgiveness is given *and* received. In other words, forgiveness is a necessary but insufficient condition for reconciliation. The individual who originally hurt you may not desire reconciliation. Then again, one or both of you may accept spiritual reconciliation, but reject an actual reunion. For instance, in the case of physical or sexual abuse, a literal reunion may be ill-advised. Perhaps a spiritual reunion alone is wisest. Jesus charged us to be as "Wise as serpents, and harmless as doves" (Matt. 10:16 KJV). How wise are we if we continue to put ourselves or our loved ones in harm's way?

A young mother who had been sexually abused by her father left her small daughter with her parents while she ran some errands one afternoon. When the grandmother stepped out to shop at a grocery store, the sexual predator-grandfather struck again. Forgiveness is beautiful; foolishness is ugly. And stupid! *Never* should we feed little lambs to vicious wolves! Nor should pardon lead battered women back into the arms of brutal beasts. Murdered voices shout: "Don't be a fool! Don't be a fool!" Forgiveness isn't a synonym for foolishness. Whether a reunion should be literal or spiritual depends on the answer to this question: "Will the future be safe?" In some cases actual reunion can be a fool's deed. Better to bridge the gulf, dissolve the barriers, and begin the long process of forgiveness from a safe distance.

The road to forgiveness is often long, with turns we cannot foresee. Nonetheless, when forgiveness comes at last, peace flows like a lazy river on a sunny day. Forgiveness heals.

After creation, reconciliation was God's first work. When sinned against by Adam and Eve in the Garden, God took the initiative to restore the relationship. In Christ, God seizes the opportunity to seek reconciliation with those who rebel

> Forgiveness isn't a synonym for foolishness.

against the love of God and love of neighbor. The apostle Paul wrote, "God was in Christ reconciling the world to Himself, not counting their trespasses against them, and entrusting to us the message of reconciliation" (2 Cor. 5:19 RSV). In the Lord's Prayer, Jesus teaches us to pray, "Forgive us our debts, as we also have forgiven our debtors" (Matt. 6:12 RSV). God forgives us, and thus we should forgive others.

Forgiveness gives us the chance to begin again. We can return to the good times. We can laugh again. Dance. Sing. Play. We can turn hurt and alienation over to God to dismiss and remove. A new future arises before us from the ashes like the legendary Phoenix. Night is over. A new day dawns. Everything changes. At least for the forgiver it does. Isaiah prophesied of the day when "the wolf will dwell with the lamb, and the leopard will lie down with the young goat" (Isa. 11:6). This new prophecy anticipates the rule of God on Earth through the Messiah, Jesus Christ. The prophecy of Isaiah finds fulfillment in the hearts of believers in Christ, while its ultimate fulfillment awaits his return. This "already–not yet" phenomenon means that each believer may have peace in his heart as he awaits God's final redemption, while the rest of creation, or any part of it, remains mean-spirited, even bloodthirsty. In the believer's heart "the wolf" may "dwell with the lamb," even though the innocent lamb dare not lie down with the unchanged wolf of the world.

Does the wolf dwell with the lamb in your heart? Why not give yourself the test of forgiveness? Are the interpersonal barriers still there? Or are you friends again? Do you wish that guy well who dumped you? Or the girl who rejected you for another? Does your blood still boil at the thought of the woman who stole your husband? Are you still bitter because your friends left you out of the big event? Are you still holding a grudge over that truth session with your best friend or your spouse? Do you still resent your parents for what they did or didn't do when you were a child? Do you still burn at the memory of the one who injured you? Or are you friends again, or at least reconciled in your heart?

Hurt, alienation, release, and *reunion* are the four stages on the journey to forgiveness. When we successfully navigate this course, we arrive at a place called forgiveness. Upon entering this land, if we listen carefully, very carefully, we can hear angels softly singing, "Welcome home. Welcome to the City of God. Welcome to the City of Peace."

5

Why Forgive?

At last the promotion was his. Dave's* wife and children were excited. Dave's parents were proud. How could anyone have anticipated what was coming? It was Sunday afternoon, and Dave was moving his office from the old warehouse district to the scenic river-lined sky-rise section of downtown. While making repeated trips from his old office to his car carrying his personal effects, he was suddenly surrounded by a gang of young toughs. Taunting him, the hoodlums began to jostle him. They shoved him, until his belongings crashed to the ground. Bending down to pick up his possessions, he arose staring eye-to-eye into the barrel of a high-powered pistol.

"Please don't shoot," he begged. "I've got a wife and two young children. I beg you; don't do it." Glancing around the circle at his fellow thugs, the gang leader sneered, then

*Not his real name.

squeezed the trigger. Pow! Blood spewing from his chest cavity, the innocent victim slammed backward onto the asphalt. Strangling on his own blood, the husband and father cried, "Please don't do it. I beg you. I've got a wife and two young children. Please." The assailant fired again. Dave was still breathing, but the gun was empty. One of the juveniles ran his hand through Dave's pants pockets pulling out his car keys. He then got into Dave's car and ran over him. Still Dave breathed. The attackers opened the car trunk, threw their prey in, and ironically, drove to the river near Dave's new office downtown, and hurled him into its dark waters. The coroner's report ruled death by drowning.

I served as pastor to Dave's mother. Arriving at the family home, I sat grieving with family and friends, helplessly listening to Dave's loved ones weep. "Would you please go and talk to my husband, Pastor?" Dave's mother pleaded. "Sure I will," I responded sympathetically. "Where is he?" "He's in the hospital. He's so filled with rage. With his bad heart and all, I'm afraid if he doesn't forgive, they're gonna kill the second man in our family."

Turning into the hospital parking lot, I worried, "Now what'll I do? Dare I go into that hospital room and ask this enraged father to forgive his son's murderers? Do I have the right to do that? What if it were my son? Could I forgive? What if he screams, 'Why should I forgive!' Then what? What do I say then?"

> *If we're honest, we must admit we could easily build a moral case against forgiving.*
> *Why should we forgive?*

If we're honest, we must admit we could easily build a moral case against forgiving. Why should we forgive? First someone steals something valuable from you—your loved one, your dreams, your dignity. Then you're asked to extend forgiveness too? We all possess a natural revulsion against forgiveness. Why be a doormat? What an outrage it is to insist that victims forgive! Isn't forgiveness an indication of weakness? "Are you asking me to excuse his actions?" we loudly complain. "Isn't forgiveness a not-guilty verdict? It's unfair!" Aren't we asking victims to hurt twice when we ask them to forgive? To ask a hurting victim to endure the pain of wishing the villain well is outrageous. It's unfair!

The world *is* an unfair place. Bad things *do* happen to good people. Can we create fairness in this world by forgiving? If offering forgiveness is unfair, what is the alternative? We can choose to reject Jesus's example and replace it with Clint Eastwood's example. Maybe when push comes to shove, force is the best answer. "Go ahead. Make my day." We can ignore Jesus's way of bearing wounds with spiritual might and return the wounds with magnum force instead. This approach, after all, refuses to tolerate what is morally intolerable. However, forgiveness can only occur in the face of morally intolerable deeds.

"I am accustomed to pay men back in their own coin," boasted Bismarck, Germany's first chancellor. Perhaps you have seen the bumper sticker, usually on the back of a pickup truck: "I don't get mad. I get even." The problem with getting even is it never happens! Revenge chains us to the whole painful event. Both feuding parties get stuck on a merry-go-round, taking turns hurting the other. The get-even proverb is a lie! Revenge is not sweet. It is a bitter poison which stuns us, drugs us, and soon kills our souls. I should confess to you here that I have tasted it. Have you? Spit it out! We drink the poison of revenge at the risk of spiritual suicide. Anne Lamott is right. Seeking revenge is "like drinking rat poison and waiting for the rat to die." An old Chinese proverb warns us, "Whoever opts for revenge should dig two graves."

Gandhi warns, "If we all live by the law, 'an eye for an eye,' soon the whole world will be blind."[1] Besides, the pain you give is never the same as the pain you get. The hill is steeper going up than coming down because your pain is compounded. You merely hurt yourself when you become a pain-giver. You cease to be Dr. Jekyll and become Mr. Hyde. The old you has turned into a fiend, and the monster within you lives to cause pain, waiting for the right moment to lunge out of the dark and attack your targeted victim. You get stuck in a painful past like houseflies on a glue strip. But there is another option: *forgiveness.*

Forgiveness is truly a miracle, first of God's grace, then of our will. Hate pulls us down a path toward self-destruction. Forgiveness opens the door to new life. Forgiveness is not about the past; it is about the future. To be sure, different paths into the future are available to us, but only forgiveness leads us to a place called peace.

Elie Wiesel paralyzes me with pain every time I read his haunting writings from the Holocaust. In *Night,* his terrifying volume of horrors chronicling his family's fate under Hitler's demonic reign, Wiesel testified that he was only a lad of twelve when he and his family were thrown into a German death camp. "Men to the left! Women to the right!" After hearing those words, Wiesel saw his mother and little

> *Forgiveness is not about the past;*
> *it is about the future.*

sister, Tzipora, for the last time. As they parted forever, he to hard labor and his mother and sister to a fiery furnace fed by innocent human beings, he watched his mother stroke Tzipora's hair as if she could somehow protect her. Wiesel alone, of his family, survived the hell of the Holocaust. After watching helplessly as SS troopers beat his beloved father to his hands and knees at Auschwitz, young Wiesel, who later became a Nobel Peace Prize Laureate, silently vowed to himself, "I will never forgive them!"[2]

Why should he forgive? Why should anyone forgive? Surely various answers could be offered by others. Nonetheless Christians should forgive for three reasons: for Christ's sake, for the sake of others, and for our own sake.

We Forgive for Christ's Sake

To be a Christian is to declare that Jesus Christ is Lord. The earliest salvation formula was just that simple (Rom. 10:9). A believer's proof, however, lies not only in one's profession of Christ as Lord, but also in the practice of Christlike living. *Is* Christ really Lord? Is he boss? Do we obey him? Do we follow his example? Do we allow the Holy Spirit to direct our lives? "Not everyone who says to me, 'Lord, Lord,'" Jesus warned, "will enter the kingdom of heaven, but only he who does the will of my Father in heaven" (Matt. 7:21 NIV).

> *To whitecapped waters of rage, forgiveness whispers, "Peace, be still."*

Clearly, forgiveness *is* the will of God. First, we are to receive forgiveness from God through Christ, then we are to forgive others. According to the Bible this is God's cosmic plan for us (Col. 1:13–14; 3:13). Why? Because forgiveness returns love to the heart—the very place from where it has leaked out. Forgiveness restores the soul. Forgiveness heals relationships. To whitecapped waters of rage, forgiveness whispers, "Peace, be still."

"In everything, do to others what you would have them do to you," Jesus taught, "for this sums up the Law and the Prophets" (Matt. 7:12 NIV). No doubt opposing ideologies compete for a believer's soul. "You have heard that it was said, 'You shall love your neighbor and hate your enemy.' But I say to you," Jesus enlightened, "love your enemies and pray for those who persecute you, so that you may be sons of Your Father who is in heaven" (Matt. 5:43–45). Then he warned: "For if you forgive others for their transgressions, your heavenly Father will also forgive you. But if you do not forgive others, then your Father will not forgive your transgressions" (Matt. 6:14–15).

The writer of Ephesians exhorts, "Do not grieve the Holy Spirit of God, by whom you were sealed for the day of redemption. Let all bitterness and wrath and anger and clamor and slander be put away from you, along with all malice. Be kind to one another, tender-hearted, forgiving each other, just as God in Christ also has forgiven you" (Eph. 4:30–32). "You are not your own," the apostle Paul admonished, "you were bought with a price" (1 Cor. 6:19–20 AMP). "You have been set free from sin and have become the slaves of God," he proclaimed (Rom. 6:22 AMP). "Never avenge yourselves" (Rom. 12:19 AMP). Rather, "if one has a complaint against another, forgiving each other as the Lord has forgiven you, so you also must forgive" (Col. 3:13 RSV). In his letter to the believers in Rome, Paul wrote,

> For not one of us lives for himself, and not one dies for himself. . . . whether we live or die, we are the Lord's. For to this end Christ died and lived again, that He might be Lord both of the dead and the living. Why do you pass judgment on your brother? . . . For we shall all stand before the judgment seat of God.
>
> Romans 14:7–10 RSV

When contemplating forgiveness, we cannot avoid the question. "*Is* Jesus Lord?" Clarence Jordan, the founder of Koinonia Farms and publisher of *The Cotton Patch Version of the Gospels*, is said to have once lamented, "We'll worship the hind legs off Jesus, then not lift a finger to do a single thing he says." Is such the case for Christians in the difficult task of forgiveness? "For if you love those who love you, what reward have you?" Jesus challenged. Then he commanded,

"You, therefore, be perfect as your heavenly Father is perfect" (Matt. 5:46, 48 RSV).

For Christians, the sacrifice Jesus made on the cross remains the paradigm for living. "If anyone wishes to come after me," Jesus said, "he must deny himself and take up his cross daily and follow me" (Luke 9:23 NIV). Paul reminded the Corinthian Christians, who were struggling to get both their theology and their morality right, that Christ "died for all, so that they who live might live no longer for themselves, but for him who died and was raised again" (2 Cor. 5:15 NIV). He continued, "Therefore if anyone is in Christ, he is a new creation. . . . All this is from God, who reconciled us to himself through Christ, and gave us the ministry of reconciliation" (2 Cor. 5:17–18 NIV).

Another way of stating this truth is to say that God is re-creating the world, sinful though it is, through Jesus Christ in the church. As Richard Hays puts it in *The Moral Vision of the New Testament*, "The church community is God's eschatological beachhead, the place where the power of God has invaded the world."[3] To clarify, he notes, "The church community is a sneak preview of God's ultimate redemption of the world." Or as Paul exclaimed, God wills that "the life of Jesus may be manifested in our mortal flesh" (2 Cor. 4:11 RSV). In short, we are called to live and forgive like Christ.

"Why Forgive?" These words jumped off the face of the January 9, 1984, *Time* magazine cover with a picture that shocked the world. With his left arm draped in fatherly fashion around Ali Agca, the Turkish gunman who had made an attempt on his life, Pope John Paul II tenderly embraced the right hand that had aimed and fired a near deadly bullet into his body on May 13, 1981. Whispering words of grace, the pope forgave his would-be assassin.

A whisper, perhaps, to Agca, the patriarch's words and action reverberated loudly around the world as an altar call to the spiritually deaf. In forgiving his young, misguided enemy, the head of the Roman Catholic Church offered a troubled, hate-filled world an unforgettable image of grace. Even among Christians, many of whom appear to be much more comfortable with Christ in print than in practice, John Paul's initiative was disarming. The church leader, known to millions of Catholic Christians worldwide as the holy father, proclaimed, "I spoke to him as a brother whom I have pardoned, and who has my complete trust." Later, addressing inmates in the prison housing Agca, John Paul elaborated, "I was able to meet my assailant and repeat to him the pardon I gave him immediately. . . . The Lord gave us the grace to meet as men and brothers, because *all the events of our lives must confirm that God is our Father and all of us are His children in Jesus Christ, and thus are all brothers*" (emphasis mine).[4]

In forgiving his potential murderer, Pope John Paul II took the Word of God to heart, giving testimony to the lordship of Jesus Christ in his life. The whole emphasis of the New Testament and Christianity is on forgiveness of sins, reconciliation, and holy living, manifested and made possible by the love of God through the sacrifice of Jesus Christ on the cross (Rom. 5:5–6; 1 John 4:9). Christians need to forgive, first and foremost, for the sake of Christ.

We Forgive for the Sake of Others

One of the most amazing prayers ever penned (now included in *The Oxford Book of Common Prayer*) was apparently written by an unknown prisoner in a German concentration camp at Ravensbruck. Found on the body of a dead child, the prayer read:

> O Lord, remember not only the men and women of good will, but also those of ill will. But do not remember all the suffering they have inflicted upon us; remember the fruits we have bought, thanks to our suffering—our comradeship, our loyalty, our humil-

ity, our courage, our generosity, the greatness of heart which has grown out of all this, and when they come to judgment let all the fruits which we have borne be their forgiveness.[5]

Oh, what a prayer! Most of us would have to confess that such greatness of soul is beyond our comprehension. But, oh my, what an example! What a spiritual goal!

Stephen, one of the servant-leaders of the first-century church, was stoned to death because of his devout faith in Jesus Christ. Standing nearby, holding the coats of those who stoned Stephen, was a young man named Saul. As the

> Saint Augustine observed later, "Had Stephen not prayed, the church would not have had Paul."

bloody martyr lay dying, Stephen breathed this prayer: "Lord, do not hold this sin against them" (Acts 7:60 NIV). In due time, the young Christian-persecutor Saul miraculously met Jesus and became the great apostle Paul. Saint Augustine observed later, "Had Stephen not prayed, the church would not have had Paul."

Some time ago I was invited to preach in a certain church on the theme of forgiveness. As I began, I immediately noticed that a particular gentleman in the congregation seemed to be hanging on every word I spoke. Not a syllable I spoke fell to the floor. He soaked up every utterance, every gesture like a dry sponge in a pail of water. When the worship service ended, the man waited in a line of well-wishers until we stood face-to-face. "Well, you're just like all the rest," he lamented, shaking his head. "You preachers are always answering a bunch of questions nobody's asking. You never even touched on the question I have!" he complained. "All you guys are the same!" "Look," I replied, "I'm sorry I didn't deal with whatever it is that's bothering you. Maybe if you tell me what you have on your mind, we can talk about it now." "Yeah, I'll tell you, 'cause you sure didn't say anything about it in your sermon," he continued. "What I want to know is this. *Do I have to forgive him if he doesn't repent?* That's what I want to know. Answer that!"

"That's a good question," I replied, "a very good question. But it's not the real question, is it?" I asked. "What do you mean it's not the real question?" he demanded. "Please don't get me wrong," I said. "Yours is a very important question. It's just not the real question, is it?" "Oh, and just what, may I ask, is the real question?" he probed. "'Do I have to forgive if he doesn't repent?' is a good question," I repeated. "But the real question, it seems to me, is, *'Can he repent if I don't forgive?'* That's the real issue." "What are you talking about?" my new friend implored. "The cross," I answered. "What's the cross got to do with it?" he demanded. "Everything," I replied. "The cross has everything to say about the way we live our lives. Think about it," I insisted. "Who had repented of the crucifixion of Christ when he forgave? Who? Pilate? The high priest? The Romans? The silent masses? The cowardly disciples? Who? No one! Yet Jesus cried out from the cross, 'Father, forgive them for they know not what they do.' No one had repented, yet Jesus forgave. And somehow our cold, hard hearts are melted in the warmth of the Son, aren't they, including my heart and yours? We are standing here today because of that unconditional love and forgiveness, aren't we?" Then I concluded, "Who knows? By forgiving your enemy he may yet repent and become all that God intends him to be." My new friend stood silent, thinking. Then ever so slowly, he turned and quietly walked away. What he did with the words he heard, I have no idea.

The question "Do I have to forgive if he doesn't repent?" deserves serious reflection. The short answer to the question is yes. Why? Because the gospel of Jesus Christ calls us to a new way of living, in light of the cross, where injuries suffered meet with unconditional love and forgiveness. In order to live this new life we need more than information, however. We need transformation. We must be born again.

The probing question "Can he repent if I don't forgive?" calls us to think seriously about the example of Jesus from the cross. Technically, of course, one could repent before being forgiven by another person. However, *God's* unconditional love and forgiveness precede and await *our* repen-

> Contrary to popular view, forgiveness precedes repentance! Repentance is the result of God's forgiveness, not the cause of it.

tance. God's grace in and through Christ on the cross finds us, saves us, and changes us. Therefore Paul wrote to the believers in Colosse, "Just as the Lord has forgiven you, so you also must forgive" (Col. 3:13 NRSV). Christian living in light of the cross means that we, like our Savior and Lord, forgive unconditionally. Sinners have their *best* chance to repent as disarming grace flows freely from Christ and his body, the believers.

The Christian's model and mandate was demonstrated at the cross. It is at Calvary, the site of Christ's crucifixion, where Christ taught us an unforgettable lesson. Contrary to popular view, forgiveness *precedes* repentance! *Repentance is the result of God's forgiveness, not the cause of it.*

God does not love us and forgive us because we repent; rather we repent because God loves us and forgives us. Paul wrote, "God proves His love for us in that while we still were sinners Christ died for us" (Rom. 5:8 NRSV). John added, "We love because he first loved us" (1 John 4:19 NRSV).

Repentance preceded *neither* God's love *nor* Christ's atoning death on the cross. Yet the innocent, sinned-against Christ forgave. Such love and grace catch us off guard. Never is love more touching than when it is unexpected, undeserved, and unconditional. When a victim responds to evil with good, the wrongdoer experiences spiritual disequilibrium. He becomes confused. He realizes he isn't getting what he deserves. He *is*, however, getting what he needs. How can that be? He is disarmed. Grace is pounding on the door. "Do I open the door or bolt it fast?" he debates. A crisis of the soul erupts. Life and death hang in the balance and the wrongdoer knows it. The gospel has found him. Competing paths diverge sharply. Each beckons. "Come this way." "No here!" He must decide whether he will journey toward the light or sink deeper into darkness.

The message of the cross calls us home. At Calvary we learn that reconciliation is the task of the victim. Of course, we are uncomfortable with the ethical implications of a theology of the cross. We who have been wronged prefer that the offender make amends. Instead, the model of Christ

> *When the Word becomes flesh, lives are changed.*

and his work on the cross portray the *injured* party taking the initiative to restore the relationship. Wrongful injury becomes an opportunity to display the life-changing grace of God. Therefore, those who are being transformed into the image of Christ should actively look for opportunities to bring God's shocking grace into moments of evil. A Christian's life can become a living Bible given to family, friends, and acquaintances. Make no mistake about it, such a life is a Bible that will be read daily. When the Word becomes flesh, lives are changed.

Years ago I read an article by Tim Noel in *Proclaim* magazine, entitled, "The Gospel According to *Gunsmoke*." Noel had found the gospel portrayed in an old *Gunsmoke* episode (*Gunsmoke* was a popular western television series in the '60s) and published his fascinating analogy. I, too, vividly recall viewing the same episode Noel saw.[6]

The outlaw in this particular episode decided that an empty church would provide a vulnerable and lucrative target for theft. After carefully choosing a deserted house of worship, the villain entered, stole the crucifix and gold candlesticks, and then turned to make his escape. As he headed up the aisle of the church, a priest walked in, surprising the thief. A single shot from the gunslinger's pistol dropped the priest to the wooden floor. As the priest lay dying, with the thief leaning over him searching for personal valuables, the victim performed a startling deed. Reaching into his chest cavity to dip his thumb in his own blood, the priest slowly lifted his hand to his killer's forehead, drew a bloody cross in its center, and whispered as he died, "I forgive you."

The thief froze. Taken completely off guard by his victim's pardon, the troubled killer departed and proceeded to roam from town to town, racing from the haunting words he could never outrun. The New Testament picture of Christ hanging from the cross, whispering, "Father, forgive them . . . ," provides the template for transformational forgiveness. As Paul preached, "God was in Christ reconciling the world to Himself, not counting their trespasses against them, and He has committed to us the word of reconciliation" (2 Cor. 5:19). What Paul's statement means is *the victim has the task of attempting reconciliation*. How revolutionary! Unlike pagan religions where the offended gods demand appeasement from the offender, the innocent Christ took the initiative to restore the broken relationship with sinful humankind. The implication stuns us. If Christ, as victim, took responsibility for the well-being of his enemies, we who claim to be Christians, or Christlike, must do the same. That is precisely what the priest in the *Gunsmoke* episode understood.

Haunted by grace, the restless outlaw made his way from town to town, fleeing from the person he could become. At one town he tried giving his stolen goods to a church, but the preacher refused to accept the items, likely realizing they were stolen. Was the thief trying to repent? Was forgiveness working its magic?

As the episode neared its end, the bad guy rode into Dodge City, home of Miss Kitty, Doc, and Marshall Matthew Dillon (the main characters of the series). All too soon the outlaw and the marshall faced each other in a showdown on the streets of Dodge. The villain drew his gun first. But Marshall Dillon drew his faster. As the lawman leaned over the fallen outlaw, the dying man whispered his last three words: "I forgive you."

"The Gospel according to *Gunsmoke!*" Not bad stuff for an old TV western, and not too farfetched either. Forgiveness can dramatically change a person's life, which may explain why sometimes "truth is stranger than fiction," as the true story that follows illustrates.

Johnny Lee Clary, Grand Dragon of the Ku Klux Klan, sat impatiently in a local radio studio awaiting the arrival of his debate opponent, the Reverend Wade Watts of McAlester, Oklahoma. Reverend Watts, head of the Oklahoma National Association for the Advancement of Colored People, served as pastor of a McAlester church, which Clary unsuccessfully had tried to burn to the ground. When Reverend Watts arrived, he walked over to the hate-filled Klansman, who defiantly sat attired in his white sheet. Extending his hand, the black minister smiled and said, "I love you." Caught completely off guard, the KKK's grand dragon reached out his own hand and embraced the minister's hand of forgiveness.

The year was 1979. Within ten years, Clary had risen to the rank of Imperial Wizard in the Klan. However, he had never been able to shake the warm welcome, smile, and loving words of his supposed archenemy. One fine day in 1989, Clary convened the Grand Council of the Klan and dropped a bombshell. "I quit," he announced. Two years later, Johnny Lee surrendered his life to Christian ministry. Testifying that he could no longer run from the haunting witness of Reverend Watts, Clary called the minister to share his good news. Watts invited Clary to preach in his church, and soon the two men were traveling throughout the south preaching a gospel of racial reconciliation, even protesting together at KKK rallies. Next Clary founded a ministry called Operation Colorblind, Inc., to combat racism. Following the death of Reverend Watts, Mrs. Watts shared, "Johnny Lee became like family to us. He always told us how much he loved us."[7]

So why do we forgive? We forgive for the sake of others. Who knows? By forgiving our enemies, they may yet repent, be transformed, and become all that Christ intends them to be.

We Forgive for Our Sake

Christians should forgive for the sake of Christ and others, but thirdly, we forgive for our sake also. Some might argue that this is a pagan appeal rather than a Christian one. I do not agree. It is certainly true that, as opposed to hedonism and narcissism, Christianity calls individuals to deny themselves, to become other-centered rather than self-centered. However, the biblical call to salvation and godly living often contains a dreadful warning intended to appeal to the best interests of the hearer. In particular, the threat of a fiery judgment in hell arouses an understandable self-interest. When Jesus told the parable of the unforgiving servant (Matt. 18:23–35), he avowed that anyone who refuses to forgive a debtor would meet with unspeakable torture. He drove home the point that among other reasons, we should forgive for our sake.

We should not, of course, forgive merely for our sake. Such theology and practice would, indeed, be pagan. An approach of this nature could perhaps be called self-help, self-improvement, or the pursuit of happiness. What it could never be called, however, is Christianity, or the pursuit of holiness. Any notion of forgiveness that focuses exclusively upon the self, caring nothing at all about God or neighbor, cannot rightly be called Christian (Matt. 22:37–39). Rather, we forgive first for Christ, second for others, and third for ourselves. But yes, we do forgive for our sake. In fact, we must!

Why must we forgive? Because forgiveness is the only way to be fair to ourselves. Only forgiveness of self liberates us from a painful past into a new future. Forgiveness sets us free from those dark, evil forces that can storm our minds, seize our souls, and hold us hostage until the ransom of revenge is paid, then paid again and again, until at last we are morally and spiritually bankrupt.

"We pardon to the degree we love," French author and essayist La Rochefoucauld observed.[8] To refuse to forgive is to choose to hate. Hatred is cancer of the soul, carcinoma of the human spirit. Hatred always kills its host. It is like a howitzer with a plugged barrel, exploding in the face of its unsuspecting cannoneer. Hatred breeds revenge. Revenge is a boomerang that clobbers the one who throws it. Like

> *Not to forgive is to choose to live backward rather than forward.*

explosives strapped to the chests of terrorists, revenge turns us into fanatic suicide bombers. We are being cruel and unfair when we bind ourselves to a torturous past. Not to forgive is to choose to live backward rather than forward. It is to prefer to be imprisoned in the past rather than be released to live freely in the present.

"But I have been violated!" an abuse victim may justifiably cry. "How is forgiveness fair? What about justice? What about judgment?" Paul Tillich once wrote, "Justice must be maintained and guilt confirmed before forgiveness is possible." Therefore forgiveness is *not* a substitute for judgment; forgiveness *is* judgment! The unfair hurt is recognized, then swiftly judged without compromise. "I judge you guilty! And, I forgive you." Though forgiveness may come slowly, when it does come, forgiveness opens the door to the possibility of fairness.

Forgiving the one who robbed you of your dignity is the *only* way to be fair to yourself. You were humiliated once. You are humiliated again and again and again when you refuse to forgive. You become a POW in your own private war for two; you are tossed into a concentration camp where the guards blocking your escape are your own brutal thoughts; you are cast upon the rack of your memory; you become a pain-junkie, popping pills of hate as you press "rewind," then "play," on your private VCR, allowing the videotape to clobber you again and again, while you relive the horror, seethe, and burn with resentment. Please don't do that to yourself! You did not deserve to be violated in the first place; you certainly do not deserve to suffer now and forever.

Only forgiveness liberates you. Unless we break with the evil past, our present and future are hopelessly overwhelmed and drained of hope. Not to forgive is to consent to become the slave of your tormentor. Your emotions, actions, and attitudes surrender to the commands of your commander. Don't look now, but you are no longer free.

Jesus offers an alternative to resentment and revenge. "In everything, do to others what you would have them do to you," he taught (Matt. 7:12 NIV). Is this the only way to live? No, not really. Of course not. We must confess that the *easiest* way to live is simply to "do to others as they *do* to you." After all, this approach merely allows you to react. You don't have to think. You just do what others do to you. They're bad; you're bad. They're good; you're good. They hurt you; you hurt them. Maybe in a moment of reflex response we find retaliation the easiest way to live. In the *long* run, however, retaliation will kill you.

When simply a responder, you cease to be a human being and become like a puppet dangling on a string. You become a slave dancing to your master's wicked fiddle, or maybe today, his happy tune. You are an automaton. Your every mood and move are programmed by another. You are a toy belonging to your cruel adversary, a yo-yo, up or down, high or low, depending on the whim of your enemy. A dictator controls you. Languishing under the spell cast by your enchanter, you grow sick. Hypnotized, you surrender your thoughts and actions to your master. Zombie-like, you sleepwalk twenty-four/seven. Don't you want to wake up and return to your true self?

Why exist as a slave, when you can live as a free person? Do unto others as you would *have* them do unto you, Jesus urged. The Golden Rule *is* the gateway to liberty. It is the secret passage to a place called peace. When we treat others the way we would like to be treated, we live on a spiritual plane above all pettiness and cruelty. We are free. Unlike caged animals left to ape those who interact with them, we are fully human and fully free. We respond with grace. We live and love on a level higher than evil can comprehend. We return good for evil, preventing or breaking the cycle of madness.

My favorite among the legends surrounding Leonardo da Vinci's masterpiece *The Last Supper* involves his archenemy. As the story goes, da Vinci determined to paint the face of his nemesis in the face of Judas at the Last Supper. This would, of course, enshrine da Vinci's adversary in infamy. The great artist carried out his scheme only to discover that for the life of him, he could not envision the face of Christ to complete the commissioned work. In a sweat-driven state of existential angst late one night, the troubled genius bolted upright in his bed knowing what he must do. Leaping out of bed and racing to his easel, he erased the face of his foe from the character of Judas. Once he altered the painting, he saw the face of Christ. Soon da Vinci completed the masterpiece known today as one of the world's finest and most loved paintings.

As it did with da Vinci, forgiveness unlocks the handcuffs of hatred and liberates us to pursue our full potential. Are you being fair to yourself when forgiveness can set you

> The question is not,
> "How can I live as though it never happened?"
> The question is,
> "How can I live now that it happened?"

free? The question is *not*, "How can I live as though it never happened?" The question is, "How can I live now *that* it happened?" Complete fairness, of course, exists only in heaven, but interpersonal forgiveness is the fairest approach in this life. We do not always have a voice or a vote in the painful events that befall us in life. Yet, we have everything to say about the kind of person we become as a result of those events.

David Lewis refused to be bitter. While serving as Bishop of Llandaff, Lewis was hanged for his Roman Catholic faith on August 27, 1679. Before marching to the gallows, this gentle man testified,

> As for my enemies, had I as many hearts as I have fingers, with all those hearts would I forgive my enemies. . . . But . . . especially do I forgive my capital persecutor, who hath been so long thirsty after my blood; from my soul I forgive him, and wish his soul well, that, were it in my power, I would seat him a seraphim in heaven. . . .[9]

Most of us fall short of the standard of grace set by Bishop Lewis.

In the Sermon on the Mount, Jesus taught his disciples to pray, then concluded: "If you forgive others their trespasses, your heavenly Father will also forgive you; but if you do not forgive others, neither will your Father forgive your trespasses" (Matt. 6:14–15 NRSV). This is a hard saying. How should we interpret Jesus's words? Some say, "Jesus meant to imply that God rewards us when we forgive others. We forgive; God forgives. We try to get others; God gets us." My response to this interpretation: Horsefeathers! God is not interested in playing games. Our heavenly Father has no desire to engage in tit-for-tat exchanges with his creatures. God's character is not dependent upon ours. Rather, our character is derived from God's. We love because God first loved us. Not the reverse. While we are yet sinners, God loves us. Whose character is primary? Whose is secondary?

Another interpretation of this passage claims that Jesus meant we will *feel* forgiven if we will only forgive others. But where does the text say anything at all about feelings? Is there another way to interpret the words of Jesus? How about taking them as *fact*?

If we share in the gift of forgiveness, then we *can* forgive; we *will* forgive. An unforgiving spirit houses pride, bitterness, and selfishness, revealing an anti-God state of mind and an absence of God. When we experience new birth in Christ, however, the result is reconciliation, as our hearts melt in repentance before God and leap to embrace our neighbor in forgiveness. Our pride and hardness of heart, which prevent us from forgiving others, on the one hand, prohibit us, on the other hand, from sincerely humbling ourselves to ask and receive God's forgiveness. Refusal to forgive is a sure indication of a heart that has not been transformed by God's grace. In sharp contrast, a forgiving spirit is home to humility, divine grace, and love, which give witness to a life dedicated to God and filled with God's presence.

God does not offer the gift of forgiveness without giving the power to forgive. If we do not have the power to forgive, then we have not received the gift of God's forgiveness. Where God's presence is, God's power is also. So the question is not, "If I don't forgive, can I be forgiven?" The question is, "If I don't forgive, *am* I forgiven?"

The best way I know to illustrate the truth of what Jesus taught is with the picture of a door. A door that is closed on one side is closed on the other side. A door that is open on one side is open on the other side. Suppose you sin against me but the door to my heart is slammed shut so that forgiveness cannot get out to you. Remember, a door that is closed on one side is closed on the other side. Therefore God's forgiveness cannot get in to me. Now suppose I wrong you. Through a

> *God does not offer the gift of forgiveness*
> *without giving the power to forgive.*

miracle of grace, the door of your heart cracks, then opens wide to let forgiveness out to me. A door that is open on one side is open on the other side. Therefore God's forgiveness can get in to you. This is what I think Jesus meant when he said that God will or will not forgive our trespasses as we do or do not forgive others.

The apostle Paul wrote in similar terms to the Christians at Corinth.

> If anyone is in Christ, he is a new creation. The old has passed away; behold, the new has come. All this is from God, who through Christ reconciled us to himself and gave us the ministry of reconciliation; that is, in Christ God was reconciling the world to himself, not counting their trespasses against them, and entrusting to us the message of reconciliation.
>
> 2 Corinthians 5:17–19 ESV

One who has become a part of the new creation community will find a way to initiate reconciliation with others. None of us is perfect. Just perfectly forgiven. So we reach out to forgive imperfect friends and family members as we, who also are imperfect, have been forgiven. We do this for Christ's sake, for the sake of others, and for our sake as well. At the end of the day, our capacity to forgive others provides reassuring evidence that *we* ourselves have received God's gift of forgiveness.

For many of us, the hardest person to forgive is ourself. The good news is that God does not expect us to forgive in our own strength. Only through God's grace in our hearts is forgiveness possible. When we are ready, grace awaits.

6

How Do We Forgive?

Ronald was attending Netterville Elementary School when I arrived in the first grade, and he was still attending Netterville Elementary School when I left for junior high. Ronald stood six foot one and weighed 155 pounds in second grade. (Okay, well, in *my* mind he did, anyway.) His developmental tasks in elementary school included shaving, driving, drinking, registering for the draft, the usual. I was three foot seven, forty-nine pounds, trying desperately to learn how to hold my pencil, repeat the alphabet, and spell c-a-t.

Almost every day as I walked to school, Ronald would pounce upon me from behind. With his trusty, tightly wound newspaper, he would beat me over the head repeatedly. Again and again his blows would rain upon my noggin. Perhaps this release was not as satisfying to him as a smoke, but cigarettes were a bit expensive for a second grader. Hitting me was Ronald's way of relaxing.

I hated the monster. He was tall, skinny, and mean. And he was ugly. It was the mean part I hated. The other stuff I figured he didn't volunteer for. When Ronald wasn't pounding my skull with his newspaper, he would kick me with his pointed-toe cowboy boots. Even today, I can still picture his evil, lanky walk, his worn-out blue jeans, pointed-toe boots, dingy T-shirt, and oily flattop haircut. How could I ever forget that greasy black comb, thick with a month's supply of pink Butch Hair Wax mixed with white dandruff flakes, sticking out of his right back, blue jeans pocket? Always, of course, he carried that horrible rolled-up newspaper.

Did I mention that I *hated* Ronald? One cruel difference between memories and actual events, I have discovered, is that memories can humiliate you forever. My guess is if you are still reading this far, you know exactly what I mean.

"As the Lord has forgiven you," the apostle Paul insists, "so you also must forgive" (Col. 3:13 ESV). Yes, but *how* do we forgive? We know *what* forgiveness is; we know *why* we

> One cruel difference between memories and actual events, I have discovered, is that memories can humiliate you forever.

should forgive; now we need to know *how*. When the weight of hate drives our weary shoulders to the ground, then what? Suppose we are ready, really ready, for the lightness of liberation? When our souls ache for the freedom of forgiveness, *how* do we forgive? I've concluded that the process of forgiveness is accomplished slowly, with understanding, humanly, divinely, specifically, without seeking revenge, sometimes in person, with prayer, Christianly, and with continued prayer. In some sense I will continue this discussion by speaking to myself, inviting you to eavesdrop.

Slowly

People forgive slowly, gradually, as a rule. We need to give grace time to grow. In the event you are blessed with miraculous grace overflowing, which enables you to forgive your offender instantly, the rest of us rejoice with you and the cheering heavenly hosts. For most of us, however, forgiveness is a struggle. It takes time. "Time heals all wounds," the saying goes. Do you agree? I do not. Such truth-claims are generalizations. Better to say, "Some wounds are healed in time; others are not." As a rule though, time does provide a better perspective on our woundedness.

A Chinese proverb reminds us, "The longest journey begins with the shortest step." It may be that our journey to forgiveness needs to begin with an honest prayer such as this: "Lord, you know it is hard for me to forgive. To be honest, I don't even *want* to! Will you help me to *want* to forgive? Maybe if you can help me to *want* to forgive, then I can take the next step, and the next, until you have helped me forgive." Forgiveness often arrives slowly.

With Understanding

When we understand our offender, or at least try to understand, forgiveness becomes easier. I said "easier," not "easy." For most of us, forgiveness is never easy. Especially when the burr under the saddle of our memory continues to rub us raw. Yet, when we make a cognitive decision to quit focusing on ourselves as victim, choosing instead to see the other person as the truly needy one or one to be pitied, it helps. What is his need? What insecurities or complexes affect her actions? What childhood circumstances or current fears influence his behavior? To be sure, to understand is not necessarily to approve. Each individual must bear responsibility for his choices. Still it helps us with our forgiveness process if we can take a step or two in the other person's shoes.

On February 3, 1998, Karla Faye Tucker became the first woman executed in Texas in more than one hundred years. Found guilty of the pickax murders of Jerry Lynn Dean and Deborah Thornton, she died of lethal injection in the Texas state penitentiary in Huntsville.

On June 11, 1983, Karla, her live-in lover, Danny Garret, and several friends began a weekend drug binge. After a couple of days of shooting heroin, smoking cocaine, and popping pills, Karla and Danny broke into Jerry Lynn Dean's apartment, where Dean and his new acquaintance, Deborah Thornton, were asleep in bed. The gruesome murder which followed repulsed the nation. The two murderers were sentenced to death, Karla on April 25, 1984.

Karla was raised in a violent home. Her father was a physically abusive alcoholic. He and Karla's mother fought often. Karla began smoking marijuana with her older sisters at the age of seven or eight. By age ten she was shooting heroin. By seventh grade, she had dropped out of school. When her parents divorced, Karla lived with her mother, who taught her the art of prostitution. Karla was fourteen. One day Karla's mother laughingly informed Karla that she was conceived as the result of an affair, deeply hurting and angering Karla.[1] As a result, Karla was haunted by this disclosure.

Karla Faye Tucker was reared in a violent world of physical abuse, alcohol and drug abuse, and sexual promiscuity. Nothing about her upbringing excuses Karla's grotesque crime. ("Guilty!" came the jury's verdict. "Death!" her penalty.) However, knowing Karla's story may at least help us to understand a little of what we probably can never fully understand. Sometimes a little understanding makes possible a lot of forgiveness.

Still the axiom "To know all is to forgive all" takes far too lightly the evil nightmares inflicted upon innocent people, especially young children who subsequently suffer a lifetime of guilt, fear, and pain.

Understanding that an abuser had a difficult childhood doesn't always move us to forgive. It may or may not prove therapeutic to seek to understand another's experiences. Suppose we discover that the person who hurt us did so in premeditated fashion, considering at length what would hurt us most. Isn't it possible that knowing all could conceivably make forgiving even more difficult?

Forgiving others becomes easier when we remember our own sinfulness, though once again, there are no guarantees. Hopefully, when we realize how much we owe God, how massive the debt is which God forgave, we will be moved to forgive the lesser debt of others. Jesus once told a story about a king and his servant. The servant owed the king millions of dollars. When the king demanded that the servant pay his debt, the servant could not do so. The debt was too great. Therefore the ruler ordered that the man, his wife, and children be sold into slavery in order that payment might be collected. The poor man pleaded for mercy and time. Having compassion upon the man, the king erased the servant's debt completely and allowed him to go free. Jubilant, the servant ran away celebrating.

On his way home, this servant encountered another servant who owed him several dollars. When his fellow servant could not pay, the debt-free underling seized his debtor by the throat and began to choke him. Although the poor second servant begged for mercy, none was granted. Instead the first servant whose debt had been forgiven by the king ordered the man to be imprisoned until the money could be paid. When the king learned what had happened, he summoned the first servant and said to him, "You wicked servant! I forgave you all that debt because you besought me; and should not you have had mercy on your fellow servant, as I had mercy on you?" Then in anger, the king sentenced the unforgiving servant to the dungeon (Matt. 18:23–35 RSV).

Forgiving others becomes easier when we realize our own sinfulness. Be that as it may, the awareness of his own forgiven debt, regrettably, did not move the unforgiving servant in Jesus's story to have mercy. Nor did the men in the Gospel of John who wanted to stone a woman caught

> *Forgiving others becomes easier when we remember our own sinfulness.*

in adultery give indication they were willing to forgive her when Jesus cautioned, "Let him who is without sin among you be the first to throw a stone at her" (John 8:7 RSV). Nonetheless, the condemning men slipped quietly away to wrestle with their own guilt.

Humanly

We sometimes forgive, but remain angry. Is that bad? Maybe. Maybe not. But it's completely human to become angry when we are offended; quite natural as a matter of fact. Sin hurts individuals and their relationships. Since acute and chronic anger harms one's cardiovascular system, rage proves ill-advised from a health perspective. Working through anger offers the more obvious, healthy choice. Moreover, unresolved anger leaves barriers in place within relationships and does nothing to heal a festering crisis of forgiveness. Even so, if the question is, "Can I legitimately be angry after I forgive?" the answer from a psychological perspective is, "Yes." An event in the past, which angered you, remains imprinted in your memory, doesn't it? Furthermore the memory's staying power is particularly strong if there has been no sign of remorse or repentance from the offender. Although unjust situations merit legitimate anger, often bitterness, animosity, and estrangement follow, as well. When this happens, darkness engulfs us. Hostility and hatred kidnap our peace and love. Friendships freeze. The world grows colder by the minute. Evil laughs. Sin wins. We lose. Consequently, Paul warned, "Be angry and do not sin; do not let the sun go down on your anger, and give no opportunity to the devil" (Eph. 4:26–27 ESV; see also Ps. 4:4).

Anger in itself is not a sin. If it were, Paul would not have differentiated between anger and sin. If anger were a sin, Jesus Christ could not be called sinless, since his anger moved him to drive out money changers from the temple (John 2:13–17). If anger were a sin, God would not be known as an angry God (Pss. 79:5; 85:5). However, God is indeed angry at sin. Occasions arise when the absence of anger may reveal a malaise of the soul. Under certain circumstances, a lack of anger is psychologically unnatural. Discrimination, for instance, calls for righteous rage. Didn't anger gain women the right to vote in America? Didn't anger result in civil rights for Black Americans? Sometimes anger at wrongdoing brings about positive social change and justice.

Anger is a legitimate human emotion. Anger is as God-given as love. Psychologically understood, anger is preceded by hurt, which in turn is preceded by love. We are touched or hurt depending on whether we receive more or less than we are expecting. If my wife expects nothing unusual this mundane Monday, but I surprise her with a box of chocolates, a dozen red roses, a dinner date, and a romantic whisper, "Happy Monday, Honey; I love you," she will be deeply touched (OK, *shocked!*). If, however, our anniversary falls on that same Monday and the day passes without any acknowledgment from me that I remember or care, she will be hurt. On a much more intense level, spouses injure each other terribly in cases of marital infidelity. Since we hurt to the degree we love, our sharpest pain inevitably comes from those we love most. No wonder our anger is often fiercest within our family units.

Set Free by Forgiveness

"I am so angry at him, I could kill him!" our friend confessed to my wife and me regarding her husband, who was also our friend. "I just cannot believe he was having an affair with that . . . for months, while living a lie, pretending to be a good father, husband, and Christian," she cried. "Was he sleeping with her and me at the same time? You bet he was!

> *Anger is a legitimate human emotion.*
> *Anger is as God-given as love.*

Ooooh! I am so . . . mad!" Sobbing, our mortified friend cried, "I don't know if I can ever forgive him! I don't even know if I *want* to!"

Was our friend entitled to her feelings of rage? Was her anger sinful, or was it just? Were feelings of malice toward her husband, or the other woman, acceptable? What, might we ask, is the difference between anger and malice? Anger is a passionate dislike for the wrong that was done. Malice is a passionate dislike of the one *doing* the wrong. Anger is legitimate. Malice signals a major problem.

In the anger scenario mentioned previously, the emotional progression flows from love, to hurt, to anger, and regrettably, sometimes to hatred and hostility. (Or from deep love to deep hurt to deep anger, etc.) Take away the love factor and the progression from anger to fury differs somewhat: A goal is blocked, causing frustration, which, in turn, leads to anger, and unfortunately, often hostility. In both types of anger, hostility threatens to spring forth from the anger. When this happens the gates of hell swing open. Pandora's Box spills its evils. Due to the frightening danger lurking around the corner from anger, Paul strongly warns of imminent sin, and the presence of an opportunistic devil any time anger rages unresolved.

Anger is a battery awaiting its charge. The charge may be either positive or negative. Anger empowers angels, but also

92

inhabits demons. We wear halos or sprout horns depending on how we respond to our anger. Love is constructive. Hate is destructive. Anger can be either. Anger is good when it hurts neither others nor self. It is bad when it attacks individuals rather than problems. Anger is godly when it redemptively unleashes energy. It is demonic when vindictive. Anger is classified as virtue or vice depending on whether it helps or hurts people. When we forgive an offender, we may find that our anger melts like an ice cube in fire. Or we may discover that our anger sizzles and remains. We are human,

> *Love is constructive. Hate is destructive.*
> *Anger can be either.*

and every human responds differently. Therefore, "Be angry but sin not" (Eph. 4:26 RSV).

Divinely

"Christianity is hard!" people frequently complain. Where do folks get such crazy ideas? Nothing could be further from the truth. Christianity is *not* hard. *It is impossible!* We cannot live Christianity in our own strength. Only by the grace and power of the indwelling Holy Spirit can we live the life God created us to live. In other words, Christians live and forgive divinely.

Jesus does not merely save souls, he also establishes a community where believers are united with him and with each other. We are "one in Christ," the apostle Paul wrote (Gal. 3:28 NIV). Appealing to the metaphor of a body, Paul illustrated the manner in which we are each a part of a larger whole (1 Corinthians 12). He also explained that a new creation becomes reality "in Christ." The church is a glimpse of what God is "up to" with humankind (Eph. 3:9–11). The death of Christ on the cross was a unique historical event, a pivot point if you will, that reconciled humankind to God. This reconciliation, when accepted, results in a new creation community. This new creation community, the church, em-

> *Christianity hard? Nonsense. It is impossible! That is why we need Christ.*

bodies the self-giving Spirit of Christ, portrayed most profoundly on the cross. Empowered by the indwelling Holy Spirit (Acts 1:8), believers give and *forgive* in the name and power of Christ. *The cross of Christ provides the model for relationships in the new creation community (2 Cor. 5:14–19), while the Holy Spirit provides the power.* Christianity hard? Nonsense. It is impossible! That is why we need Christ.

Love is the mother of forgiveness. Without love forgiveness will never be born. "Love bears all things, . . . hopes all things, endures all things," the apostle Paul reminded the contemptuous, divisive Christians at Corinth (1 Cor. 13:7). "Owe no one anything, except to love each other" (Rom. 13:8 ESV), Paul wrote on another occasion to the believers in Rome. "The commandments . . . are summed up in this sentence," he proclaimed. "'You shall love your neighbor as yourself.' Love does no wrong to a neighbor; therefore love is the fulfilling of the law" (Rom. 13:9–10 RSV). As an engine is to an automobile, so love is to forgiveness. Without love, forgiveness goes nowhere.

Love gives birth to forgiveness, but not just any kind of love. One kind of love says, "I will love you *if* you meet my needs or fulfill my expectations." Such love is conditional love. Conditional love says that when and only when favorable conditions are met, love results. Since forgiveness is only necessary under unfavorable circumstances, the "if" kind of love can offer no help with forgiveness whatsoever. Love has quite logically evaporated. A second kind of love says, "I love you *because* you meet all my needs and requirements." This type of love is *competitive*. Unfortunately, it is also a catalyst for anxiety. Whoever does the best job of meeting my needs receives my love. Love dies when the "because clause" falls to the ground unfulfilled or is better fulfilled by another. When love is dead, forgiveness cannot live. In short, to say, "I will love you *if* you always make me happy," or "I love you *because* you never fail me," is to insure both a failed relationship and one which can never be repaired.

Only a divine kind of love holds relationships together. Only a Christ kind of love restores broken friendships. Only a God type of love proves *unconditional*. To insure stability and forgiveness, love must commit *regardless*. Love must absorb the unpleasant. It must be unconditional. Such love says, "I love you no matter what; I love you in spite of; I love you no strings attached." This is precisely the way God loves us. The biblical word for this divine love is *agape* (ah-GAH-pay). "It is" as Swiss theologian Emil Brunner put it, "not a love that judges worth, but a love which bestows worth."[2] It is a giving love, and a forgiving love, on behalf of others. *Agape* is a love based upon the character of the one doing the loving, not upon the merit of the one being loved. Rooted in the subject, rather than the object, *agape* is therefore unaffected by conditions. Love, *agape*-style, never ends (1 Cor. 13:8).

Agape is the New Testament Greek word that is translated "love" in each of the following passages of Scripture:

- "God is love" (1 John 4:16).
- "We love, because He first loved us" (1 John 4:19).
- "God shows his love for us in that while we were still sinners, Christ died for us" (Rom. 5:8 ESV).
- "God's love has been poured into our hearts through the Holy Spirit who has been given us" (Rom. 5:5 ESV).

- "The fruit of the Spirit is love" (Gal. 5:22 NIV).
- "If someone says, 'I love God,' and hates his brother, he is a liar" (1 John 4:20 NKJV).
- "I give you a new commandment: that you should love one another. Just as I have loved you, so you too should love one another" (John 13:34 AMP).

A Christian's call and capacity to love *unconditionally* comes from God. What God expects us to be, God empowers us to be: agents of grace and reconciliation. *Agape* is the genius of Jesus's death on the cross and the life to which we are called. Yet Jesus's crucifixion is not the last word. The resurrection, empty tomb, ascension, coming of the Holy Spirit, and our repentance and receipt of all God offers complete the drama. As Christians, we then walk in the way of Christ by means of God's guiding commandments, the example of Christ, and the empowerment of the Holy Spirit. Flannery O'Conner once acknowledged, "You shall know the truth and the truth shall make you odd." Well, the truth is, God calls us *and* empowers us to live a life of *agape* love, which indeed makes us odd, odd like God.

Specifically

In seeking to forgive, we need to be specific as to what we need to forgive. Focusing on one matter at a time helps us in two ways: First, with laserlike precision, we can vent our feelings. Venting our hurt and anger to the wrongdoer may help restore our diminished self-respect. Verbalizing our hurt, our humiliation, our rage to a friend or counselor may also help with the healing process. Certainly, venting to God is imperative. We should always tell God how we honestly feel about life's ups and downs. Second, confining our focus to one problem at a time, we can resist the temptation to demonize our adversary. Each of us is loved by

God and created in God's image. Therefore we should see the person who wronged us as good. We are not forgiving an individual's entire existence. We are forgiving the specific wrong done.

Consider trying the following experiment as an illustration of specificity: Draw a single black ink dot the size of an aspirin in the center of an otherwise all white sheet of paper. Ask a friend, "What do you see?" "I see a black dot," is almost always the answer given in reply. Ah-ha, the trap is sprung! A standard sheet of white paper measures 8 ½ x 11 inches! Yet inevitably we focus on the small black dot. What about all the white? Aren't we guilty of making the same sort of mistake with good people who do bad things? It is difficult *not* to dwell on the dark deed.

Without Seeking Revenge

When someone wrongs us, we hurt, become angry, and often seek revenge. With fantasies of payback dancing in our heads, forgiveness never sets foot onto the dance floor. To forgive we must give up the idea of getting even. Alas, human nature houses other ideas. "I cannot believe she did what she did," the former office manager complained. "She went behind my back to make me look bad to the others in the office. She lied. She schemed. She intentionally plotted my failure. I had no chance to be successful," the victim angrily shared. "I know this is crazy," she confessed, "but I dream of paying her back someday. What I really want to do is to get her fired—see who gets the last laugh then!"

When revenge is present, forgiveness is absent. Healing can only begin when we give up the dreams of nightmares for our enemy. By contrast, engaging in restoring a relationship with the offending person advances wellness for both parties. Suppose the fired office manager in the previous scenario is later rehired as a vice president of the company due to a change in ownership. Furthermore, suppose she demands that the woman who had wronged her report to her immediately. "Debbie, I want you to know that I know everything you did behind my back five years ago. Your actions were tragic for both of us. You hurt us both. I lost my job; you lost your character. You were wrong, terribly wrong to do what you did. Debbie, I forgive you. I want to offer you a promotion, a chance to help me take this company to new heights. I believe you have immense potential for good around here, personally and professionally. What do you say? Can I count on you?"

Revenge or restoration? Which is more likely to make both parties better persons?

Sometimes in Person

The subhead for this section does not read, "In Person," but rather, "*Sometimes* in Person." Sometimes a heart-to-heart session with your offender opens the door to healing. Other times a truth session makes matters worse. The key question is: By going to this person, will I make matters better or worse?

A Christian is never in a position of privilege, no matter if wronged or the wrongdoer, such that he or she is excused from the responsibility of working for reconciliation. God personally gave us a model of a victim who forgave in Jesus's words on the cross. The victim in God's model took the initiative to restore a broken relationship. God gave us *only* the model of a *victim* because God can *only* be sinned against; God cannot sin. Therefore, we don't have a picture of God seeking forgiveness for having transgressed. Surely, however, when *we* wrong God or neighbor, we should rush to seek forgiveness. As Jesus directed, "So if you are offering your gift at the altar, and there remember that your brother has something against you, leave your gift there before the altar and go; first be reconciled to your brother, and then come and offer your gift" (Matt. 5:23–24 RSV). The larger context

> A Christian is never . . . excused from
> the responsibility of working for reconciliation.

leaves little doubt that Jesus is placing the initiative for reconciliation squarely upon the shoulders of the wrongdoer. Thus *all* are accountable—victim and villain—for doing the hard work of forgiveness and reconciliation. We might even go so far as to admit that in many broken relationships, vindication of complete innocence versus determination of sole blame is not an easy task.

Matthew 5:23–24 teaches us that Christ is less concerned with our religion than our relationships. His command to leave worship to repair relationships echoes the emphasis of the prophets Amos (Amos 5:21–24), Hosea (Hosea 6:6), Isaiah (Isaiah 58), and Jeremiah (Jer. 7:4–7). Bible scholar W. E. Vine puts it well, "Love can only be known by the action it takes."[3]

A few years ago a pastor friend of mine accepted an invitation to teach in a church out of state. On the last night of his engagement, an attractive woman in her late thirties asked to visit with him for a few moments following the evening worship service. He agreed. As they sat in the sanctuary afterwards she shared her painful story with him.

"I am married with two children," she began. "Recently my husband and I decided to remodel a room in our home. So we hired a local carpenter to do the work. I'm a stay-at-home mom. So while my husband and children were away at work and school, I was home during the remodeling," she related. "Things started innocently enough," she shared. "I would take the carpenter a cold coke to drink. He always thanked me. Then we would stand there talking until he finished his coke. Just being social. You know. Well," she explained, "soon we were sitting and talking at the kitchen table while he drank his coke. The breaks got longer; the looks got stronger. Then it happened," she confessed. "One day we ended up in the bedroom."

"I think I've got the picture," my friend said. "How do you think I can help you?" he asked. "Well," she replied, "I feel so guilty. I'm a Christian and he's not. I'm afraid I've hurt my witness." Then she sighed, "I haven't seen him in weeks now. I just wonder if you think I should go and witness to him. I know he's lost. What should I do?"

"I'm so sorry," the minister said. "I know you're hurting on many levels, bless your heart; but I think your answer lies in one word." "You do?" she asked. "Yes ma'am, I do," he replied.

"What is it then?" Pausing, he whispered, "Geography." "Geography?" she puzzled. "I don't understand." Softly the pastor repeated, "Geography is your answer; you need to put a whole lot of it between you and him."

What does Jesus mean when he teaches, "If your right eye causes you to sin, pluck it out and throw it away; . . . if your right hand causes you to sin, cut it off and throw it away" (Matt. 5: 29-30 RSV)? Surely he does not mean for sinners to engage in self-mutilation. We would all wear patches and hooks! Besides, most of us could find a way to sin left-handed, or lust with our remaining left eye. Rather Jesus means we should separate ourselves from whatever causes us to sin. For that reason the pastor assured his distraught confessor that God could find a man to witness to her carpenter friend. However well-intended, she should keep her distance.

Normally, proper action taken when we are estranged leads to improved relations, not further damage. If approaching someone would be a fool's deed, however, then we should substitute a literal visit with a spiritual approach utilizing prayer alone.

We should always take time to pray before going to another in hopes of repairing a damaged relationship. God's help will surely be needed. Sometimes sending a letter preceding a visit paves the way for a fruitful conversation. Whether the communication begins with a letter or a personal visit, sharing our pain honestly will reveal the depth of our relationship. However, we must be careful neither to criticize nor condemn the person with whom we wish to restore a relationship. Either, or both, will trigger his defense mechanisms. Instead of tearing down walls, criticism and condemnation strengthen barriers. Nor should we self-righteously announce, "I forgive you." Our friend or family member will only hear the offensive translation, "I blame you." A better approach might be to say, "I want you to know how much our relationship means to me. Our estrangement hurts me deeply. I wonder how we might work together to make things right. I want you to know I care and that's why I came."

One Sunday, Sarah Walker marched down the aisle at the close of the morning service to pray with her minister as the choir sang the invitation hymn "Just as I Am." As the two prepared to pray, the parishioner whispered, "I have hated you for a year. I just want you to know I forgive you." "You *what?*" Reverend John Harris whispered back. "I have hated you ever since you railroaded that business meeting in order to bring your friend on staff a year ago," she confided. "Anyway, I just feel God wants me to forgive you." As the congregation and choir praised God with heavenly melody, the pastor tuned around to the minister of music and said, "Keep singing!" Turning back to face his penitent church member, the clergyman protested, "The church calls her ministers, not the preacher. I never railroaded any business meeting." "Yes you did too! I heard that train whistle," Mrs. Walker bristled. "Anyway, I forgive you; let's pray!"

On the way home from church that day, Barbara Harris asked her husband, "Are you alright, Hun? You haven't spoken a word since we left church." "Yeah, I'm fine," he replied curtly. "Hun-neey, you can tell me," she halfway sang. "Okay, you won't believe it," he erupted. "Did you see who came forward in the invitation?" "Yeah, sure. Why?" "Well, do you know what she said? I'll tell you what! She said, 'I have hated you for a year!' Can you believe that?" he growled. "Said she just wanted me to know she has decided to forgive me. Hated me for a year. A *year*! What do you think about *that*!" he grumbled. "Now *she* feels relieved, and *I've* got a crisis of forgiveness!"

Sometimes silent pardon is wiser than public forgiveness. When the person you need to forgive knows nothing of the problem, more harm than good may come from a truth session. Options beg careful consideration. Conversation, of course, may indeed promise the smoothest road to reconciliation. If not, we should practice private forgiveness.

With Prayer

When we choose to engage a person directly regarding a strained relationship, we will want to pray together with that person before parting. Prayer *to* God, *with* the person, *for* the person and yourself invites God into the relationship. Thanking God for the relationship, while seeking God's forgiveness for any misunderstanding, introduces grace into our pain. God can make the relationship better than ever. All things are possible with God.

What do we do though when it is best *not* to approach the individual who causes us pain? Pray. We still pray. What do we do if the one who has hurt us terribly is deceased? Pray. We still pray. Remember, forgiveness happens to the one doing it. We need to forgive others, living or deceased. We must let go of our pain and hatred. The question becomes: Where do we put our hatred while we are on our knees in prayer? We lay it at God's feet. If we have not tried prayer, we have not tried God's way of dealing with our problem. No matter what, we still pray.

Christianly

We *choose* to live "Christianly." Treating others well, speaking graciously of them, and living life positively requires faith, hope, and love, as well as a healthy dose of wisdom. When I say we "choose" to live a certain way, questions arise. Can forgiveness be willed? Forgetting cannot; can forgiveness? We cannot make ourselves forget. Can we actually will away our anger and resentment? Emotions cannot be programmed. Isn't resentment a moral emotion? Is it within the power of the will to say, "I will not resent what you did"? Or to say, "I will feel good about you"?

William James, the noted Harvard psychologist, spoke and wrote about what we might call the "As If" principle. Recognizing that *emotions* could not be programmed, James argued that the will should guide human *actions*. Actions *can* be programmed; emotions follow. Feelings can be compared to a caboose on a train; the will functions as the engine. James recommended that we go ahead and act "as if" a desirable reality already exists.[4] Suppose a strained relationship is in intensive care. We can act "as if" wellness prevails. For example, we may not *feel* like sending a card, speaking a kind word, or purchasing a friendship gift. However, by *willing* healing actions such as these, our emotions soon stand transformed. *We may not be able to will forgiveness, but we certainly can will the steps which lead to forgiveness.*

Transformation often surprises us and the other person as well. Through the darkness of a fallen world, the sages of old guided Israel into the bright light of practical wisdom. "If your enemy is hungry, give him bread to eat; and if he is thirsty, give him water to drink; for you will heap coals of fire upon his head, and the LORD will reward you" (Prov.

25:21–22 RSV). From this ancient book of wisdom comes enlightenment: Warm acts of compassion melt ice. "Heaping coals of fire upon his head" refers to the shame felt by an enemy who receives mercy. "The reward from the LORD" refers to peace, internal, interpersonal, or both.

In his book *Lincoln on Leadership*, Donald Phillips notes that Lincoln was "slandered, libeled, and hated perhaps more

> We may not be able to will forgiveness, but we certainly can will the steps which lead to forgiveness.

intensely than any man ever to run for the nation's highest office." Phillips relates that Lincoln was called "a grotesque baboon, a third-rate country lawyer who once split rails but now splits the Union, a coarse vulgar joker, a dictator, an ape, a buffoon, and the craftiest and most dishonest politician that ever disgraced an office in America."[5]

Two of Lincoln's harshest critics were William H. Seward and Edwin M. Stanton. Yet, Lincoln, believing in the two men's abilities, appointed the former Secretary of State and the latter Secretary of War. Later Seward wrote his wife, "The President is the best of us." Following Lincoln's assassination, Stanton mourned deeply, saying, "Now he belongs to the ages."[6] Warm action melts cold hearts.

In writing guiding words to the believers in Rome, Paul quoted the passage cited earlier from the book of Proverbs and then added, "Do not be overcome by evil, but overcome evil with good" (Rom. 12:21 NIV). Likewise, in teaching his disciples (in the Sermon on the Mount) how to live "Christianly," Jesus acknowledged, "You have heard that it was said, 'You shall love your neighbor and hate your enemy.' But I say to you, love your enemies and pray for those who persecute you, so that you may be sons of your Father who is in heaven" (Matt. 5:43–45).

In a gracious move signaling goodwill to the South at the end of the Civil War, Lincoln ordered that "Dixie" be played at a White House rally. Offering a verbal olive branch, the president announced, "I have always thought 'Dixie' one of the best tunes I have ever heard." Later, in his second inaugural address, Lincoln spoke graciously "with malice toward none; with charity for all." Lincoln was so reticent to execute a soldier accused of cowardice in battle, so determined to forgive, that he once observed, "If Almighty God gives a man a cowardly pair of legs, how can he help them running away with him?"[7]

Grace transforms. I once read a story of two men who had been enemies for years. One became ill. Somehow through a miracle of grace—who knows how this happens—the other man brought meals to his enemy every day. How long do you think they remained enemies?

With Continued Prayer

What is the secret to godly living? Prayer. "Pray for those who persecute you," Jesus taught. "Pray like this," he encouraged, "Forgive us our trespasses, as we forgive those who trespass against us" (Matt. 6:12 KJV). Paul, too, urged, "Rejoice in your hope, be patient in tribulation, be constant in prayer" (Rom. 12:12 ESV). Prayer is the antidote for the universal human disease "Hardening of the Hearteries." The related malady "Bacillus Enemyosis" responds well to prayer also. Prayer is penicillin for sin sickness. Prayer is chicken soup for the soul.

"It's hard to hate someone you're praying for."

As a child, when I found the temptation to return meanness with hatred far too strong to resist, Mother would ask, "Have you prayed for him?" "Have I *prayed* for him?" I

105

would protest. "I don't want God to *bless* him; I want God to *get* him!" Then Mother would remind me, "It's hard to hate someone you're praying for."

Mother's kneeology has never been replaced by any theology I have found. Whenever we suffer from a crisis of forgiveness, we will become, in the long run, either bitter or better. *We all make choices about the kind of person we wish to become.* Genuine prayer in the spirit of Jesus transforms us into beings of love. As we pray for our antagonist's best, for his well-being and success, we journey from the gates of hell to the streets of heaven. The chariot that transports us there is prayer.

7

Forgiveness from God

Everyone has a dark side. We all are sinners. "If God were not willing to forgive sin, heaven would be empty" (German Proverb).[1] God provides a solution to our problem of sin by offering us forgiveness. Freely.

Confession is not a condition of forgiveness; it is the path which leads there. Here's another way to look at it:

> *"If God were not willing to forgive sin,
> heaven would be empty."*

forgiveness knocks; confession opens the door; and repentance keeps the door propped open. God does not forgive our sins *because we* have repented; rather we repent *because God* has forgiven our sins. Paul wrote, "God demonstrates His own love toward us, in that while we were yet sinners, Christ died for us" (Rom. 5:8). While hanging on the cross Jesus prayed, "Father, forgive them, for they know not what they do." Simply put, there is nothing we must first do to earn God's forgiveness. In fact, there is nothing we *can* do to merit divine forgiveness. God has forgiven us through Christ's sacrifice of himself on the cross alone. Otherwise even our inaction could, and would, prevent God from forgiving us. The hope of the world would rest in God's goodness second, and in human goodness first, which ironically, has established itself as the problem in the first place. Among humans "there is none who does good, there is not even one" (Rom. 3:11–12 NIV). Thankfully, our hope rests not in the human race, but in God's grace. Even in our badness, God loves us and forgives us; he suffers with us and for us. God's unconditional love is what the cross is all about.

Through Christ's death, God has forgiven us. But we must individually accept that forgiveness through confession. "Everyone who calls upon the name of the Lord will be saved," Paul announced (Rom. 10:13 RSV). However,

> God does not forgive our sins
> because we have repented; rather we repent
> because God has forgiven our sins.

God cannot be mocked. Jesus warned, "Not everyone who says to me 'Lord, Lord,' will enter the kingdom of heaven, but he who does the will of my Father Who is in heaven" (Matt. 7:21 AMP). Only those who come to God with a sincere and humble heart will find him. God's forgiveness awaits behind the door we have closed with our pride. Our humble confessions and repentance open the door to God's forgiveness. Nobel Peace Prize Laureate Bishop Desmond Tutu of South Africa explains the receipt of unconditional forgiveness with an analogy.

Imagine you are sitting in a dank, stuffy, dark room. This is because the curtains are drawn and the windows have been shut. Outside the light is shining and a fresh breeze is blowing. If you want the light to stream into that room and the fresh air to blow in, you will have to open the window and draw the curtains apart; then that light which has always been available will come in and air will enter the room to freshen it up. So it is with forgiveness.[2]

Ralph Wood, Baylor University professor of religion and literature, tells the story (whether apocryphal or not, he doesn't know) of Karl Barth, who once was fielding a question regarding a hypothetical meeting with Adolf Hitler. Given the opportunity to speak with the brutal destroyer of peoples, what would Barth have said? Would he have

> *Only those who come to God with a sincere and humble heart will find him.*

pronounced "scorching prophetic judgment"? The great German theologian and pastor replied that his message to the Führer would have been none other than Romans 5:8: "While we were yet sinners, Christ died for us." Is there any other hope for our redemption?

Paul offered God's good news to all humans, "There is now no condemnation for those who are in Christ Jesus" (Rom. 8:1). Each of us has tasted the fruit of the Forbidden Tree. In choosing to sin, each of us has lost Eden. Most of us have learned the hard way that sin and Paradise are mutually exclusive. Confined to exile in the wilderness, while living daily under the threat of death, we long to return to Paradise. We yearn for another chance to partake of the fruit of the Tree of Life. Oh, to be able to return!

The Genesis story reminds us, as cherubim with flaming swords guard the way back to Eden and the Tree of Life, that whoever chooses to dine at the tree bearing the fruit of death cannot feast on the fruit of life. These choices are self-contradictory. Is there no second chance? No way home? No hope for Paradise regained?

In the New Testament we are introduced to a new Tree of Life. The new tree was planted on a hill called Golgotha. All of us who eat freely of the fruit of this new tree will live and never die. We will return home; we will enjoy Paradise regained. What is the fruit of the cross? It is the body and blood of our Savior, who died to save us from our first selection of fruit. *Yes, we have a second chance.*

A Second Chance

Those willing to admit the need for a second chance stand in good company with the saints in Scripture. Abraham is known as the father of the faith for the world's three major monotheistic religions: Judaism, Islam, and Christianity. (His son Ishmael, by Hagar, became the father of the Arabs, many of whom practice Islam; his son Isaac, by Sarah, carried forward the line of the Jews, from which Christ came.) Yet, Abraham misrepresented the truth about his relationship to Sarah, claiming her as his sister instead of as his wife, when Abimelech wanted to add her to his own harem. Fearing death because he was her husband, Abraham failed in his faith as he had previously when he chose to father a child by a woman other than Sarah. Once more Father Abraham's faith faltered when he laughed at God's promise to give him a son by Sarah in their old age. Abraham was a good man; but he was not perfect.

The great prophet Moses, leader of the exodus and the one to whom God revealed the Ten Commandments, murdered an Egyptian, then hid the body in the sand. Moses dejectedly roamed the wilderness for forty years before at last accepting God's call to begin again. Sometimes it takes a while for us to forgive ourselves and accept God's forgiveness.

110

Jacob, father of the twelve tribes of Israel, tricked his blind, aged father out of the blessing intended for his twin, Esau. Samson, for all his physical strength, was a weakling in willpower in the area of sexual sin; harlots and promiscuous foreign women seemed irresistible to him. David, of whom the Lord said, "This is a man after my own heart," committed adultery with Bathsheba, then conspired successfully to have her husband, Uriah, killed. Rahab, who eventually came to be named as one of the heroines of the Bible (Hebrews 11), had at one time been a harlot. Mary Magdalene, who became so close to Jesus that he appeared to her first after the resurrection, had seven demons cast from her. Even the great apostle Paul, at one time, persecuted Christians, putting many to death. Peter, of whose faith Jesus said, "Upon this rock I will build My church" (Matt. 16:18), denied Christ three times on the eve of his crucifixion. Has there ever been anyone, other than Christ himself, who had no need of confession, repentance, and a second chance?

God's Forgiveness Formula

How do we receive God's forgiveness? Paul answers, "For by grace you have been saved through faith; and that not of yourselves, it is the gift of God; not as a result of works, so that no one may boast" (Eph. 2:8–9). Any time anyone is saved or forgiven, it is by *grace*. God doesn't owe us anything. We have been given a copy of the rule book. We defiantly choose to break

> God doesn't owe us anything.

God's rules. Since we all choose to eat of the "Tree of Death" rather than the Tree of Life, God's gift of forgiveness and new life can only be seen as grace. Therefore let me first emphasize that forgiveness from God flows from a heart of grace. Grace was offered from the cross as Jesus prayed, "Father, forgive them, for they know not what they do" (Luke 23:34 RSV).

We all know what it is like to be thirsty. Most of us could also testify of our experiences with both physical and spiritual thirst. Once in Vietnam, my company went without water for three days. We fought dehydration in the stifling heat of Southeast Asia. I had "cotton mouth" so bad that I pulled enough cotton out of my mouth to weave two new T-shirts and a pair of socks! How well I remember the moment a chopper reached us with liquid life! Never will I forget the touch of that cool wet water upon my parched, cracked lips and my dry, begging tongue. How my soul giggled as I drank until my legs filled to the brim.

Chemically, water is two parts hydrogen and one part oxygen. Separately, hydrogen is a highly flammable gas; and oxygen is an absolute prerequisite for fire. Yet when put together in precisely the right fashion—two parts hydrogen and one part oxygen—these elements form a compound, not to *cause* fire, but to *put out* fire. Mind-boggling work by the Master Chemist!

All of life celebrates the gift of water. Without it, life on Earth would disappear. Water makes life on Earth possible just as forgiveness makes everlasting life possible. As with water, precious essentials come together to form God's formula for forgiveness. Water quenches physical thirst, but only forgiveness can quench the thirst of the soul.

Consciousness of Sin

The apostle John wrote in a letter to his community of early Christians,

> If we say that we have no sin, we are deceiving ourselves and the truth is not in us. If we confess our sins, He is faithful and righteous to forgive us our sins and to cleanse us from all unrighteousness.
>
> 1 John 1:8–9

In this passage John reveals the essentials of what I refer to as "God's Forgiveness Formula." With God's gift of forgiveness fully understood as a result of Jesus' death for our sins (1 John 2:1–2), John explains how we might receive God's forgiveness. The "formula" is easy to remember: C + C = C. Of course, no such formula could possibly hold up in mathematical equations, nor in a chemistry lab. In the lab of life, however, the formula works to perfection.

The first C in "God's Forgiveness Formula" stands for consciousness of sin. One of the verses quoted from 1 John warns, "If we say that we have no sin, we are deceiving ourselves and the truth is not in us." In order for us to appropriate God's forgiveness, it is imperative that we first become aware of sin in our lives. We must understand the problem before a solution makes sense.

To ask us to be conscious of our sins is to issue no easy assignment. The modern mind has an aversion to the concept of sin. Discussions of immorality have largely been replaced with conversations advocating tolerance. Talk about the "new morality" is in vogue, although it remains unclear how the new morality differs from the old immorality. We often speak of what is socially unacceptable, politically incorrect, or morally debatable. Anyone engaged in deviant behavior, our culture insists, is a product of his circumstances, a child of his environment, or a victim of society. Sometimes we shrug off immorality, sighing, "Boys will be boys. Girls will be girls." We concede that we all make mistakes, but no one seems to sin anymore. Our criminals are "sick"; our politicians commit "youthful indiscretions"; our extramarital trysts are "meaningful relationships." We bury sin under an avalanche of euphemisms.

This lax moral climate is not a new development. One prominent psychiatrist, Karl Menninger, published a book entitled *Whatever Became of Sin?* In a similar vein, *Newsweek* magazine printed an article titled "Pick and Choose Christianity." The thinking seems to be that a cafeteria-style approach to Christianity is evolving before our very eyes. Today we "take what we want and leave what we don't." Apparently what we are leaving behind is the traditional doctrine of sin. Although the study cited by *Newsweek* was limited in scope and is now dated, two statistics illustrate a valid concern. Only 57 percent of those surveyed accepted the traditional notion that all people are sinful. Fully one-third of the respondents said they may make many mistakes, but they certainly are not sinful. One typical respondent allowed, "The day that I die, I should merely have to say to my maker, take me, not forgive me."[3] Whatever became of sin?

Our challenge is to accept our guilt. Only when we have an understanding of our guilt can we experience God's grace. We must dare to be guilty. Only when we realize we are wrong can we be made right. The problem with discarding the doctrine of sin is that the doctrine of salvation goes with it. In short, no sin, no Savior.

The shortest distance between two points is honesty. Let's

> *The problem with discarding the doctrine of sin is that the doctrine of salvation goes with it. In short, no sin, no Savior.*

be honest. As fallible human beings we not only commit sins of the flesh (actions) but also sins of the spirit (heart). Let's consider two examples of sin, one from each of the categories of spirit and flesh within our galaxy of transgressions: greed and sexual promiscuity, respectively. According to a World Bank study cited in Ron Sider's *Rich Christians in an Age of Hunger*, three billion persons, half of the planet's population, live on less than two dollars a day, while 1.3 billion of those exist on less than one dollar a day. A staggering thirty-four thousand children die daily of hunger and preventable diseases.[4] Being well acquainted with such disparity, Gandhi noted, "There is enough in our world for everyone's need, but not enough for everyone's greed."

According to Gallup polls, the percentage of Americans who think premarital sex is wrong dropped from 68 percent in 1969 to 39 percent in 1996. In the eighteen to twenty-nine age group, 74 percent believe premarital sex is acceptable. Almost half of all babies born in 1992 to baby busters (those born between 1965 and 1983) were delivered to unmarried mothers.[5] Of course, we are all guilty of sexual sin. Jesus proclaimed that anyone who has lusted has at heart already committed adultery (Matt. 5:27–28).

Sins of disposition haunt our homes. We hold members of our family hostage, committing emotional blackmail with temper tantrums. We detach emotionally, withholding the love others need from us in order for them to thrive. We are guilty of sins of omission as well as sins of commission. Many things I should *not* do, I do; many things I *should* do, I do *not* do. Need I confess how infrequently I heed the biblical mandate to feed the hungry, clothe the naked, and visit the sick and imprisoned? Moreover, pride, anger, lust, envy, greed, slothfulness, and gluttony constitute a list of seven deadly sins, each of which know me by name.

Attitudes, as well as actions, may be sinful. Isn't the saying true? "Sow a thought, reap a deed; sow a deed, reap a habit; sow a habit, reap a character; sow a character, reap a destiny." Thought shapes destiny. "For as he thinketh in his heart, so is he" (Prov. 23:7 KJV).

Many of our thoughts swirl around our thirst for power and "stuff." Thoughts of materialism crowd out thoughts for God. Our homes are cathedrals dedicated to the glory of a rival god called mammon (material wealth). We lust for things, more than we long for God. Our idolatrous thoughts become meditation. Meditation becomes worship. Worship becomes more and more pagan, as it centers around the false gods of success, family, money, career, hobby, or self.

Of the Ten Commandments, the first given is the first shattered: "You shall have no other gods before me" (Exod. 20:3 NIV). Ever wonder why this commandment stands first? When this one goes, all ten stand in peril. When the anchor breaks, the ship drifts. Will neglect for God's rights lead to disregard for our neighbor's rights? Will community collapse? With God out of the way, how soon will it be before we live in a world with a population of one? "*My* will be done!" becomes our mantra. Our souls atrophy as self-centeredness grows within us like a malignant tumor. Our souls suffocate in a vacuum of selfishness. Self-absorption leads to self-destruction. Isn't all sin uncontrolled selfishness rearing its ugly head? Isn't sin the antithesis of God? Godliness gives; god*less*ness grabs. God is life; sin is death. Ironically, in becoming self-centered, the self loses. Life is lost.

Biblical writers drew upon many different words and concepts to describe what sin is like. The ancient Hebrews, however, used three main word pictures to depict human guilt. The mildest of these three is *iniquity*. The term means "to wander away," or "to go astray," as a small lamb might wander from its flock and become lost. The second term is *sin*. This word means "to miss the mark," as when an archer

> *Our souls atrophy as self-centeredness grows within us like a malignant tumor.*

takes aim, releases an arrow, but misses the target. The strongest word for sin is *transgression*. This word means "rebellion." A word picture for transgression calls to mind a bull or goat, lowering its head and angrily charging its boundaries. All of these terms imply that we, like lambs, sometimes go astray; at other times, like a determined archer, we try hard to achieve excellence, but fail; while in still other instances, we aggressively rebel against God's expectations for our lives, and falter.

Most of us would admit that we sin in all of these ways. Karl Barth, in fact, insisted that we should speak of the "man of sin" rather than the "sin of man." Why? Because, he argued, we do not simply *commit* sin; we *are* sinners! Moreover, since "the wages of sin is death" and we cannot save ourselves, we writhe in deep distress. "A drowning person cannot pull himself out of the water by his own hair," Barth exclaimed.[6] Someone else has to do it.

Many who have claimed God's salvation struggle with yielding to God's control over their lives. Isn't there, conceivably, a major difference between a *professing* Christian and a *practicing* Christian? What does it mean to say that Jesus is *Lord*? Put differently, is it not possible for me to live as a *practicing* atheist, although a *professing* atheist I would never claim to be? Aren't Christians often guilty of living daily lives as though God doesn't exist? When we leave God out of our decisions, our work, our struggles, our relationships, our joys, our pain, don't we leave God out of our lives? Does an hour on Sunday compensate for a week of neglect? We should ask ourselves, "Do I have a religion or do I have a relationship with God?"

Confession of Sin

In "God's Forgiveness Formula," where C + C = C, the first C represents *consciousness of sin*. The second C represents *confession of sin*. John explained, " If we say that we have no sin, we are deceiving ourselves and the truth is not in us. If we confess our sins, He is faithful and righteous to forgive us our sins . . ." (1 John 1:8–9). Is there any way to experience God's forgiveness other than this? *First* we must be conscious of our need for forgiveness. *Then* we must take action by confessing our sins. Suppose we were to become aware of a threat to our lives, but were unwilling to remove ourselves from the danger. How would knowledge of the threat help us? Suppose we realize suddenly that our house is on fire. Would awareness of the peril benefit us if we refuse to act upon that knowledge? We might as well sleep unsuspectingly. Wouldn't the results prove the same? Likewise our estate becomes none the richer when we know a lottery prize awaits our claim, yet we decline to come forward to accept the prize. Knowledge without action is empty.

One of the most frustrating experiences of my early years in the pastorate came in the wee hours of the morning, during a drunken, tearful visit from an abusive husband and derelict dad in my community. Awakened by a pounding on the door well past midnight, I arose groggily, opened the door, and found my inebriated guest crying uncontrollably. "Preacher, I've gotta talk to you. I just can't stand it anymore." "Come on in, come in, come in. Bless your heart, what's wrong? Here, have a seat right here. Why don't you tell me all about it?" "Preacher, I can't go on like this. Look at me! Drunk. No good! Beat'n my wife 'n' kids. I'm not worth anything, preacher! Not worth anything!"

My guest cried long and hard. An hour, maybe an hour and a half later, my visitor, who was scorned throughout the community as the local deadbeat reprobate, still resisted accepting God's forgiveness and new life. "Why don't you give God your life? Let God forgive your sins, and give you a brand-new start?" "Naw, I can't do that!" "Sure you can. Why don't we pray together right now? Let's ask God to forgive you of all those sins, and ask Christ to save you, give you peace and a new start? What d'ya say? Why not repent, and let Jesus wipe the slate clean? Aren't you ready to do that?" Nothing doing.

Confession differs from acknowledgment. Being conscious of our sin is one thing; confessing it is another. To confess our sin means we agree with God that our behavior is wrong. To repent of our sin means we give it to God so he can help us to change. Cognition of wrongdoing is prerequisite to confession, not synonymous with it. Can't we suffer the guilt of knowing our sin, minus any intention of changing our ways? Guilt is not grace. Remorse is not repentance. My nocturnal caller named his sins, yet despite his immense shame and my best efforts, the poor, tormented soul refused to forsake those sins. He just could not, or would not, repent and accept forgiveness. The table was set, but my famished friend went away starving.

Whenever the Bible equates confession and acknowledgment of sin, or confession and repentance, it is because the context implies a forsaking of sin for worship of God. One

> *Being conscious of our sin is one thing; confessing it is another.*

sinner put it this way: "I acknowledged my sin to You, and my iniquity I did not hide; I said, 'I will confess my transgressions to the LORD'; And You forgave the guilt of my sin" (Ps. 32:5).

My tragic parishioner, on the other hand, illustrates painfully that we may be quite conscious of our sins without taking the vital next steps of penitent confession and repentance. To repent of our sins means to turn around and go in a different direction. To genuinely confess our sins is to do so with the intent of forsaking them. Instead of following temptation down the path leading away from God, we turn around and come back to God. We come home. Although two paths beckon—the way of life and the way of death—only one road leads home. Let us beware the destination of the dark path! An old Chinese saying warns: "Unless you change directions, you may end up where you are headed."

Cleansing from Sin

What now? Competing for our souls, two roads lead to opposing destinies. From the narrow way wanting wear, angels sing, "Come, live." Down the wide road well-worn, the snake fibs, "Come, you will not die." Do you remember Robert Frost's closing lines in his poem "The Road Not Taken"?

> Two roads diverged in a wood, and I—
> I took the one less traveled by,
> And that has made all the difference.[7]

The path taken, which makes all the difference, is marked by *consciousness of sin*, plus *confession of sin*, which leads to *cleansing from sin*. This road leads to life. This is the way to forgiveness. In "God's Forgiveness Formula," where C + C = C, the final C represents *cleansing from sin*. "If we say that we have no sin, we are deceiving ourselves and the truth is not in us. If we confess our sins, He is faithful and righteous to forgive us our sins and to *cleanse* us from all unrighteousness" (1 John 1:8–9, emphasis added).

I cannot speak for anyone else, but there are times when I find myself at odds with family members, friends, colleagues, or God, yet stubbornly refusing to try to restore the relationship. I have learned the hard way that three days is about as long as I can hold out as a miserable stinker. The pain of alienation casts me into an inhospitable ICU, where demons, not doctors, inject me with meanness, not medicine. Thank goodness for the great Physician! His prescription? Penicillin for the soul: prayer, confession, and forgiveness.

Maybe you know what I am talking about. Read the surprising confession of one psalmist:

> When I kept silent about my sin, my body wasted away
>   through my groaning all day long.
> For day and night Your hand was heavy upon me;
>   my vitality was drained away as with the fever heat of
>   summer.
>
> Psalm 32:3–4

Apparently you and I are not the only ones who know what it's like to resist repenting of our sins. Even one of the writers of Scripture suffered the disease of pride and rebellion. Does that, ironically, give you hope? It does me. If the *psalmist* struggled spiritually, surely there is hope for me. Continue reading the testimony and encouragement of our fellow struggler:

> I acknowledged my sin to You,
>   and my iniquity I did not hide;
> I said, "I will confess my transgressions to the LORD";
>   and You forgave the guilt of my sin.
> Therefore, let everyone who is godly pray to You in a time
>   when You may be found.
>
> Psalm 32:5–6

The psalmist obviously wrestled with a sin problem, but confessed it and received forgiveness. The word *forgave* in the text means "to lift up, to bear, to dismiss, to send away." When we confess our sins, God completely removes them. As a launched satellite disappears into outer space, so our sins vanish forever. "As far as the east is from the west, so far has He removed our transgressions from us" (Ps. 103:12).

Our English word *guilt* comes from an old Anglo-Saxon word *gylt* meaning "to pay." The Bible leaves no doubt that our sin debt must be paid. Romans 3:23 asserts that we are all guilty. However, the required payment is death. "For the wages of sin is death, but the free gift of God is eternal life in Christ Jesus our Lord" (Rom. 6:23). The good news is we have a choice. *We* can try to pay for our sins, *or* we can let Christ pay for them.

In Flannery O'Conner's novel *Wise Blood*, Hazel Motes cared nothing at all about Christianity, holding the church in strong contempt. Haze was a lad of ten when he learned the circus was coming to town. Although the church held no appeal for him, he exhibited particular excitement at the prospect of seeing the "SINsational" naked lady in the sideshow. When the day of the big event came, Haze managed to finagle his way into the show. As he arrived home later, his mother met him in the yard with a stick, demanding, "What you seen? What you seen?" Admitting nothing, Haze received a whack across the legs with the stick, along with some strong preaching. "Jesus died to redeem you," she lectured.

When his mother left, guess what Haze did? He sat down, took off his shoes, and filled them with sharp rocks and small stones. Then he laced his shoes up tightly and walked a mile through the woods until he came to a creek. Taking his bruised, lacerated feet out of the shoes, he held them in the cool sand for awhile. Then he laced his shoes up tightly again and walked back home.

As Haze grew into manhood, his intense dislike for the church and Christ only worsened. He decided to start his own church. "I believe in a new kind of Jesus," he said, "one that can't waste his blood redeeming people with it, because he's all man and ain't got any God in him. My church is the Church Without Christ!" In Haze's church there was only one truth: "Jesus was a liar." A good place to seek converts, he thought, was the movie house. So Haze went to the movie house, parked his car where he could easily be seen, stood on the hood of his car as people streamed out of the movie, waved his arms wildly, and hollered like a country evangelist trying to save souls. "Come join my Church Without Christ!"

In time another fellow began parking near Haze to mimic him. Hazel seethed. One night Haze followed the man in his car. On a lonely road Haze rammed his enemy's automobile from behind. When the man got out of his car, Haze ran over him. Then he backed over the body.

This time Haze's wrong far exceeded viewing a naked lady in a sideshow. So what did Haze do following the murder? He walked to a supply store, bought a sack of quicklime, returned to his apartment, and blinded himself, cramming the lime into his eyes by the handfuls. He filled his shoes with shattered glass and sharp rocks. He wrapped strands of barbed wire tightly around his waist, middle torso, and chest

> *Every sin we commit must be paid for.*
> *Either we will pay for our sins,*
> *or we can let Christ pay for them.*

until warm blood oozed from the punctures. He wore the barbed wire like an undershirt beneath his outerwear, even sleeping in the vest of nails. Finally, suffering from influenza, Haze limped in his glass-lined shoes out into the night of an icy rain, choosing a drainage ditch for his bed. Two days later he was dead.[8]

What was Flannery O'Conner trying to say in her bizarre novel? I must admit that I do not know for sure. However, the story makes a powerful statement, from my point of view. It seems to me, the moral of the tale is that *every sin we commit must be paid for*. Either we will pay for our sins, or we can let Christ pay for them. Guilt extorts a price that, one way or the other, must be paid. If we so desire, we can reject Christ. Then we will bear the punishment of our own sins. The choice is ours.

Forgiveness for God

ewis Smedes tells the story of a poor tailor who is walking out of a synagogue when he meets a rabbi:

"Well, and what have you been doing in the synagogue, Lev Ashram?" the rabbi asks. "I was saying my prayers, rabbi." "Fine, and did you confess your sins?" "Yes, rabbi, I confessed my little sins." "Your little sins?" "Yes, I confessed that I sometimes cut my cloth on the short side, that I cheat on a yard of wool by a couple of inches." "You said that to God, Lev Ashram?" "Yes, rabbi, and more. I said, 'Lord, I cheat on pieces of cloth; you let little babies die. But I am going to make you a deal. You forgive me my little sins and I'll forgive you your big ones.'"[1]

Hmmm. Ever felt that way? Maybe, maybe not. However, when that baby is *our* baby, when the suffering is *our* suffering, when the loved one is *our* loved one, we may find ourselves crying out, "My God, why have you forsaken me?"

Forgiveness *from* God provides the solution to our dark side, forgiveness for our own sin. However, we all bear wounds from hurts we've received in life due to the sins of others. And, in our honest moments, many of us blame God for those wounds. Should we then talk about forgiveness for God?

My good friends Tom and Ethel Logue watched in cruel agony as their son Tommy died a slow, painful death following a heroic battle with muscular dystrophy. As the father of a dying son, Tom struggled with his faith. In an entry in his diary published later as a book entitled *God, Could You Talk a Little Louder?* Tom lamented,

> I have fasted, Lord. I have prayed. I have read everything on healing I can get my hands on. I have pleaded. I have begged. I have bargained. But, Tommy continues to deteriorate.
>
> I want to believe, Lord, You would—if You could—heal our boy.... All of a sudden, I'm doubting Your omnipotence. If You could, if You would . . . but You won't . . . what kind of God are You, anyway?[2]

Tom's words speak for thousands of parents who have cried an ocean of tears during the unspeakable horror of losing a child. We are shocked, however, to know that similar words were spoken from the mouth of Jesus as he hung on the cross: *"Eli, Eli, lama sabachthani?"* "My God, My God, why have You forsaken Me?" (Matt. 27:46). *Why* are

Forgiveness comes hard when we feel deserted.

we shocked? Wasn't Jesus human? He was God-in-flesh, of course, but human nonetheless. Aren't we mortals entitled to our honest feelings in the midst of our own crucifixions?

Where *is* God when we need the all-powerful one? Where? Our reasoning runs something like this:

A *loving* God would not *want* evil to harm his children. An *all-powerful* God would not *let* evil harm his children. However, evil strikes God's children every day. Therefore, God is either not loving, or not all-powerful, or neither.

The cold hard truth is that many times when we feel we need God most, he appears to be no help whatsoever. American author H. G. Wells remarked acidly, "Our God is an ever-absent help in our time of need." The daughter of a missionary once wept as she told me that her father sexually abused her for more than ten years. "Where was God?" she demanded. Forgiveness comes hard when we feel deserted.

When we look to the cross, there we find God. Crucified. Killed by our sins. Crying. Dying. There he is, right where we like to keep him—on the cross. On the other hand, when we or our loved ones suffer innocently, while it seems God does nothing about it, we may find ourselves writhing in a crisis of forgiveness. Why does a loving God let evil befall his children? What kind of God would do that? Why does God sometimes seem so powerless? For many, the title of a little book by Pierre Wolff poses an urgent question: *May I Hate God?*

In the play *The Trial of God* by Nobel Peace Prize Laureate Elie Wiesel, the entire Jewish community in the village of Shamgorod was exterminated, with the exception of an innkeeper and his daughter. When three itinerant actors ar-

Why does a loving God let evil befall his children?

rive at the inn, Berish the innkeeper insists on putting God on trial for allowing his children to be butchered. The three guests become the jury; Berish prosecutes the case; but who will serve as the defense attorney for God? A mysterious stranger named Sam suddenly appears and volunteers.

"I want to know why he is giving strength to the killers and nothing but tears and the shame of helplessness to the victims," Berish rages. Accusing God of cruelty and indifference, the innkeeper fumes, "Either he dislikes his chosen people or he doesn't care about them—period! . . . In both cases he is . . . guilty!" Would a father stand by quietly, silently, and watch his children being slaughtered? For Berish, God must bear responsibility for the death of the innocent. Sam, however, gallantly defends God, while offering one traditional defense after another for God. In the end, the identity of the *one* person willing to defend God, though the defense is a mockery of piety, is revealed: Sam is Satan![3]

Should God be defended? In the face of evil and innocent suffering, *is* it possible to let God off the hook? German theologian Jurgen Moltmann insists that "all Christian theology, and all Christian life is basically an answer to the question which Jesus asked as he died."[4] If Moltmann is right, then what response might be given to that critical question, "My God, my God, why have you forsaken me?" We too may cry out to God, "Why did you desert me in my hour of need?" "Why did you leave me all alone?" "O God, why did you let this happen?"

Despite grasping Wiesel's thesis in *The Trial of God* that there *is* no acceptable defense of God in the face of rape and slaughter of innocent victims, and that only an evil being would offer any defense at all, it seems only fair to me that other opinions be heard. God yearns for honest, open, intimate expression of our genuine thoughts, feelings, questions, and doubts; *no* person may stand between God and another human being to block such sacred, intimate conversation. Nor should lively debate be silenced.

Wiesel's voice, which serves as a beautiful model for honest expression, must summon other voices rather than suppress them. He is right, in my mind, to insist that there is nothing spiritual about plastic platitudes, canned clichés, and syrupy, superficial spiritual-speak in the face of evil. Nor should we presume to solve the mystery of innocent suffering, made all the more perplexing given our truth claims regarding God's goodness and might. "The riddles of God are more satisfying than the solutions of man," wrote English author G. K. Chesterton. Moreover, we need to realize that when our loved ones are hurting, they want our presence, not our preaching. They need their wounds dressed, not their mysteries addressed. Our suffering friends need salve, not sermons. They need grace, not gobbledygook. Love nurses. Yakety-yak curses. Silence in the face of suffering is not only golden; it is sacred. Be that as it may, when we stand in the distance, far removed from immediate nightmares, there is much food for thought. When we are tempted to blame God for the horrors of life, we might first want to consider several propositions.

God Suffers with Us

First, we need to realize that God suffers with us. Moltmann was right when he insisted that only a suffering God can help us.[5] We always suffer to the degree we love. God loves us and suffers with us. God isn't a disinterested spectator, but rather he is an active participant in our lives. Doesn't

> *Whenever evil engulfs God's children,*
> *tears fall from heaven.*

the sacrifice of Jesus on the cross prove as much? Surely the incarnation and crucifixion reveal the heart of God. Who, but one who loves us, would enter into our world, participate in our suffering, and provide for us heaven on the other side of hell? Jesus loves the little children, and we who believe are all children of God. Whenever evil engulfs God's children, tears fall from heaven.

God Must Make Choices, Too

Second, we need to realize that even God must make choices. We who believe in an all-loving and all-powerful God eagerly testify, "God can do anything!" But is that right? Isn't it better to assert, "God can do anything *that can be done*"? Some alleged possibilities prove self-contradictory and therefore impossible. For example, consider this riddle:

> If God can do anything, can he make a rock so big that he can't pick it up? Yes, God can make a rock that big! Then he can't do "any" thing, because he couldn't pick it up. Oh yes, he could pick it up! Then he can't do "any" thing, because he couldn't make it that big.

Round and round the riddle goes. Why? Because these are self-contradictory terms, the fulfillment of which is simply impossible. Likewise, we might ask, "Can God make a square circle?" Of course not! Such is a logical impossibility. God could make the finest square, or the perfect circle, but not even God can make a square circle.

So it is with free will and the sovereignty of God. Could God create us perfectly *free* and, at the same time, *guarantee* that we would always be good? Surely God could program us in robotic fashion to always choose correctly. Would we be free, however? On the other hand, God could choose to create us free. Might not freedom, then, lead to bad choices?

> Most of the evil on the planet
> results from man's inhumanity to man.
> God is not the problem; we are the problem!

Given the choice, God chose to create us free human beings. By giving us power to make choices, God voluntarily (for now) limits his control over us. Certainly as God's creation

130

Forgiveness for God

we will give an account to our all-powerful Creator and Judge on the day of reckoning. In this life, however, we are free to choose between good and evil.

It is only fair to say that although God is ultimately responsible for creating a world where evil may touch innocent people, God had a choice to make: In short, would humans be free or not? Not even God could create humans *both* free and *not* free at the same time. The terms are simply self-contradictory. So which would it be? Free humans or not? Most of us would agree that God's choice to create us free was a good one. Our free choices, however, are *not* always good. Adam and Eve chose rebellion. Cain chose evil. Are we any different? As Ivan said to Alyosha in Dostoyevsky's *The Brothers Karamazov*, we have all eaten the apple, and are eating it still.[6] Most of the evil on the planet results from man's inhumanity to man. *God* is not the problem; *we* are the problem!

God Tries to Prepare Us

Third, we need to concede that throughout the Bible, God goes to great lengths to prepare us for this grim reality: In a free world sin happens; *bad things do happen to good people*. Abel was a good person. ("The LORD had regard for Abel" [Gen. 4:4].) Yet Abel was murdered by his brother. Joseph, beloved of his father and God, was sold into slavery by his brothers and taken away to a far country. Innocent newborn Hebrew boys were murdered as they were born in Egypt in the time of Moses's birth. Jeremiah and Micaiah ben Imlah, good and faithful prophets of the Lord, were beaten and thrown into prison, respectively, for prophesying God's Word. Regarding Job, God said, "For there is no one on earth like him, he is blameless and upright, a man who fears God and shuns evil" (Job 1:8 NIV). Yet Job suffered the loss of his ten children, his health, wealth, and reputation.

131

Hosea served God faithfully. Still, his wife committed adultery and had children by other lovers. Habakkuk cried out in helpless frustration, "How long, O LORD, will I call for help, and You will not hear? I cry out to You, 'Violence!' Yet You do not save" (Hab. 1:2). Jesus's apostles suffered martyrdom. Some were stoned. Simon Peter, tradition has it, was crucified upside down. Later, Paul, who said, "I can do all things through Christ who strengthens me," could not escape the guillotine. Nor did he actually try. Paul understood reality. He was Paul, not Pollyanna. Evil happens, even to the best. Surely Paul was one of the best. Then there's Jesus the Christ, God's Son, spotless, pure innocence, perfect goodness, being of love—what about his destiny? Mocked. Spat upon. Beaten. Scourged. Murdered on a cross. Indeed, as the Bible testifies, God goes to great pains to show us the ugly reality of a fallen world.

Bad things do happen to innocent people. In a *Peanuts* comic strip, Linus and Charlie Brown sit on a brick wall. In the first frame Linus moans, "Sometimes I feel that life has passed me by." Next frame, Linus only sighs. In the third frame Linus asks, "Do you ever feel that way, Charlie

> *Bad things do happen to innocent people.*

Brown?" In the final frame Charlie Brown replies, "No, I feel that life has knocked me down and walked all over me."[7]

Understandably some insist, "Life is not fair." Others answer, "No, life is fair. Sooner or later it gets all of us." What do you think? *Is* life fair? Does God see to it that justice prevails in this life?

In his Pulitzer Prize–winning play *J.B.*, Archibald MacLeish deals with the problem of injustice, suffering, and faith in poignant fashion. J.B.'s daughter is raped and murdered. His son is killed. Another daughter is crushed to death, and two other children are killed by a drunk driver. Still J.B. believes that the innocent fare well, while sinners are punished. From his pain he utters, "God will not punish without cause. God is just." Sarah, J.B.'s wife, cries hysterically, "God is just? If God is just our slaughtered children stank with sin, were rotten with it! Oh my dear! My dear! My dear! Does God demand deception of us? Must we be guilty for Him?" In a terribly moving scene, Sarah, leaving J.B., moves toward the door,

> No one believed God was present at Golgotha.
> Yet God has never been anywhere
> quite like he was at Calvary.

stops, turns, and sobs, "I will not stay here if you lie—Not if you betray my children. I will not stay to listen. They are dead and they were innocent. I will not let you sacrifice their deaths to make injustice justice and God good!" J.B. responds, "We have no choice but to be guilty. God is unthinkable if we are innocent." At the end of the play, Sarah comes back home to J.B. who asks pitifully, "Why did you leave me alone?" Sarah replies softly, "I loved you. I couldn't help you any more. You wanted justice and there isn't any. Only love."[8]

Certainly there was no justice in what happened on the cross. Only love. No justice. Only undeserved suffering. While enduring the mockery, cruelty, and shame of the cross, Jesus screamed, "My God, My God, why have You forsaken Me?" (Matt. 27:46). How did we miss that?

God Is with Us Always

God was eerily silent at the cross. No one believed God was present at Golgotha. Yet God has never been anywhere quite like he was at Calvary. Perhaps this is the *fourth* word we should receive. We need to realize God is with us *always*, even when, and especially when, we suffer! The writer of the Twenty-third Psalm prayed: "Even though I walk through the valley of the shadow of death, I fear no evil, for You are with me" (Ps. 23:4). After the Philistines seized David in Gath, he testified, "In God I have put my trust, I shall not be afraid. What can man do to me?" "This I know," he said, "God is for me" (Ps. 56:11, 9). Alas, not all are convinced.

In the movie *Sophie's Choice*, based upon the novel by the same name, Sophie and her two children, a firstborn son of nine and a daughter of three, maybe four, are herded onto cattle trains and sent speeding toward Auschwitz. At Auschwitz an SS trooper forces Sophie to choose between her son and daughter. Only one will live. The other must die! She cannot choose. Screaming madly, as the Nazi soldier orders both children to die, Sophie yells hysterically, "Take my daughter, take my daughter." The little girl cries helplessly, "Mommy, mommy, mommy," and disappears forever. Afterwards, Sophie cries to her friend Stingo,

> I knew Christ had turned his face away from me. And that only a Jesus who no longer cared for me could kill those people that I loved and leave me alive, with my shame. Oh, God saw I went to that church. And I took the glass and knelt down and cut my wrist. I didn't die, of course. Of course not.

Sadly, Sophie later succeeded in taking her life.

How I wish the Sophies of the world could realize what Christ is really teaching with his meditation on the cross! Hurt comes to us all, yes. It is okay to be honest with our

Jesus's other name is Emmanuel, "God with us."

questions, our feelings, our doubts, yes. It is okay to cry out in soul-wrenching anguish, yes. But "please, please, please, do not walk out in the middle of the movie!" God would surely want to say, "I have *not* forsaken you. *I love you!* Sooner or later everyone suffers. That is the terrible contract of a fallen world. Everyone is terminal. Death comes to all. Sin kills. But *this* I promise: Evil will *not* have the last word! *Stay with me!*"

Stay with me? As if we could ever get away from God!

> Where can I go from Your Spirit?
>   Or where can I flee from Your presence?
> If I ascend to heaven, You are there.
>   If I make my bed in Sheol, behold, You are there.
> If I take the wings of the dawn,
>   if I dwell in the remotest part of the sea,
> even there Your hand will lead me,
>   and Your right hand will lay hold of me.
>
> Psalm 139:7–10

Jesus's other name is Emmanuel, "God with us." That is the promise and person of our Lord. God is with us always.

God Has a Plan

God has a plan? What might that plan possibly be? In a word: *redemption!* We need to believe that the God who created this world free, even to be filled with evil, acts to redeem it. This is the *fifth* truth to remember.

The major motifs in God's cosmic drama are creation, fall, redemption, and consummation. Or to alliterate: *creation, corruption, correction,* and *consummation.* Since God's good creation has freely chosen sin and corruption, God acted in Christ to correct the problem. "God was in Christ reconciling the world to Himself" (2 Cor. 5:19). "If anyone is in Christ, he is a new creature; the old things have passed away; behold, new things have come" (2 Cor. 5:17). God is re-creating the world through Christ in the church. Once we become a new creation, "the love of Christ controls us" (2 Cor. 5:14).

Christians are then charged with leading others to receive new life in Christ (2 Cor. 5:19–20). In this way, one by one, the world is being re-created. Will this work ever become reality? Is history moving toward a goal? Will the consummation of the dream come to pass? Our answer comes in Revelation, the final book of the Bible:

> Then I saw a new heaven and a new earth; for the first heaven and the first earth had passed away . . . "Behold, . . . God Himself will be among them, and He will wipe away every tear from their eyes; and there will no longer be any death; there will no longer be any mourning, or crying, or pain; the first things have passed away." And He who sits on the throne said, "Behold, I am making all things new." And He said, "Write, for these words are faithful and true."
>
> Revelation 21:1, 3–5

These words soothe our broken hearts, unless of course, our enemies also benefit from God's grace. Sometimes we have a difficult time forgiving God for allowing our adversaries to prosper. Do we not? We watch in bitter resentment as they fare well. Jonah was unable to forgive God for his *goodness* to the people of Nineveh. The storyteller related,

> God relented concerning the calamity which He had declared He would bring upon them. And He did not do it.
> But it greatly displeased Jonah and he became angry. . . . [Jonah] prayed to the LORD and said, ". . . I knew that You are a gracious and compassionate God. . . . Therefore now, O LORD, please take my life from me, for death is better to me than life." The LORD said, "Do you have good reason to be angry?"
>
> Jonah 3:10–4:4

Truth be known, God is terribly hard to forgive when bad things happen to us, *and* when *good* things happen to our enemies. Job complained, "The earth is given into the hand of the wicked" (Job 9:24). Job blamed God for the success of evildoers. Don't we do the same? When our enemies succeed, we die a little. Sometimes God has to be forgiven for his goodness.

When Jesus cried out from the cross, "My God, My God, why have You forsaken Me?" he was referring directly to a christological psalm, one which looked forward in time. Moreover, by quoting the opening line of Psalm 22, Jesus was following a rabbinical custom of pointing to a block of material by simply introducing it. He was in effect saying, "Buy the book and read it. Here's the title." Rest assured, Jesus's question was indeed heartfelt. Those feelings were painfully his own. However fleeting the thought may have been, Jesus felt deserted by God. Yet, he pointed to a psalm that all but ends in a hallelujah chorus!

> For He has not despised nor abhorred the affliction of the
> afflicted;
> nor has He hidden His face from him;
> but when he cried to Him for help, He heard. . . .
> The afflicted will eat and be satisfied;
> those who seek Him will praise the LORD. . . .
> All the ends of the earth will remember and turn to the LORD,
> and all the families of the nations will worship before You.
>
> Psalm 22:24, 26–27

Jesus was at once both asking and answering the question, "Why have you forsaken me, God?" The silent answer was "I haven't." This event tells us there is triumph on the other side of tragedy. Nothing is too big for our God. God, not evil, has the final say. Jesus is victor, not victim. Jesus was teaching that it is perfectly alright to think our thoughts and feel our feelings. Since the sinless one asked, "Why?" can questioning God be a sin? May we not also question, complain, and doubt? God desires honest communication. God yearns for authenticity in our prayers. Dishonesty is sinful; honesty is sacred.

Does God ever forsake us? No. Do we ever feel like God forsakes us? Yes. When we harbor negative thoughts, we might as well voice them to God since he knows them anyway. Ultimate faith is not believing that because we love God bad things will never happen to us. Rather, ultimate faith is believing that *when* life is unbearable—*when* the night is the darkest,

> ### Does God ever forsake us? No.
> ### Do we ever feel like God forsakes us? Yes.

when evil is the strongest, *when* hope is the dimmest—God is *present*, not absent, working to bring about resurrected life!

Paul wrote, "Christ has been raised from the dead, the first fruits of those who are asleep. . . . Death is swallowed up in victory. O Death, where is your victory? O Death, where is your sting?" (1 Cor. 15:20, 54–56). Who is this one that brings new life out of the deepest darkness? "Thanks be to God," the apostle exclaimed, "who gives us the victory through our Lord Jesus Christ" (1 Cor. 15:57). Although he was beaten, flogged, stoned, left for dead, and eventually beheaded for his faith in Christ, Paul confidently proclaimed,

> Who will separate us from the love of Christ? Will tribulation, or distress, or persecution, or famine, or nakedness, or peril, or sword? . . . In all these things we overwhelmingly conquer through Him who loved us. For I am convinced that neither death, nor life, nor angels, nor principalities, nor things present, nor things to come, nor powers, nor height, nor depth, nor any other created thing, will be able to separate us from the love of God, which is in Christ Jesus our Lord.
>
> Romans 8:35–39

We need to be clear about one fact. Jesus did not die, as some have said, asking, "My God, why have You forsaken Me?"

He died whispering, "Father, into Your hands I commit My spirit" (Luke 23:46). Honest questions to begin; total trust in the end. When we find ourselves on cruel crosses, we may consciously or subconsciously blame God. Might we then not have a crisis of forgiveness with God? If so, we should be honest with God and honest with ourselves. We will certainly want to keep the lines of communication with God open. Some things we may never understand. Still, questions are good. Doing the hard work of trying to uncover answers is laudable. Grace is also good. Investigation takes us only so far. Never will we attain total intellectual understanding of the deepest mysteries. When we arrive at the end of the road, the candle flickers, then goes out. The rest of the journey winds through wilderness and darkness. We walk by faith, not sight,

> *Perhaps there is something better than understanding God after all—trusting him.*

or we go no farther. Yet a voice calls us forward. Who knows? Perhaps there is something better than understanding God after all—trusting him. Color that grace. Or faith. Better yet, consider it "by grace through faith" that we find our way out of the darkness into the light.

Could it be that God's answer to the question, "My God, My God, why have You forsaken Me?" is simply, "I haven't"? Even so, do we dare put words in God's mouth? The epigram reminds us that "Silence is God's first language—everything else is a poor translation."

Ah, but faith hath ears eye hath not seen. Faith hears when no word is spoken. Silence invites us to deeper levels of listening. Has God *ever* spoken louder than he did at the cross? *Listen!* In the deafening silence at Calvary comes a whisper in the wind. Do we hear what I *think* we hear? *God is often present most, where he appears to be least.*

9

Forgiveness for Others

One of the hardest things we are called on to do is forgive. We naturally resent anyone who harms us or harms those we love. We seethe. Resentment demands the ransom of revenge. We live to "pay them back." With our words or with our deeds, maybe both, we will get them. We think, *Just you wait!*

The "Impossible" Task

Now is the time for some good news and bad news regarding forgiveness. First the bad news: Forgiving others is not simply hard. It is *impossible!* The good news? What is impossible with us is possible with God! Thomas Long, professor of preaching at Emory University, stated this paradox well:

> The New Testament is always calling us to do what we cannot do—to love our enemies, to bless those who persecute us, to

141

pray without ceasing, to be perfect as God in heaven is perfect. The New Testament commands us to live these impossibilities because what is impossible with human beings is possible with God; because we are promised that, as we put one foot in front of the other to seek to live out these commands, what is commanded of us is given as a gift.[1]

The power to forgive comes from God and is available to us through prayer.

Corrie ten Boom suffered humiliation and degradation at the hands of Hitler's Nazis during World War II. Unlike millions of others, including members of her own family, Corrie survived the death camps. After the war Corrie spoke often of the need to forgive one's enemies. Following a church service in Munich, a former SS trooper approached

> *The power to forgive comes from God and is available to us through prayer.*

her. Corrie recognized him as a guard from Ravensbruck. "How grateful I am for your message, Fraulein," he beamed. "To think that, as you say, he has washed my sins away!" With that he reached out his hand. Corrie froze. Keeping her hand to her side, she fought back surging anger from haunting memories. Vengeful thoughts raced to the surface of her mind. In her book *The Hiding Place*, Corrie recalls what happened next. "Lord Jesus, I prayed, forgive me and help me to forgive him." Still her hand would not move. "Jesus, I cannot forgive him. Give me Your forgiveness," she begged. "As I took his hand the most incredible thing happened," she explained. "From my shoulder along my arm and through my hand a current seemed to pass from me to him, while into my heart sprang a love for this stranger that almost overwhelmed me." Listen to what Corrie concluded:

And so I discovered that it is not on our forgiveness any more than on our goodness that the world's healing hinges, but on His (Christ's). When He tells us to love our enemies, He gives, along with the command, the love itself.[2]

Some years ago the Gallup Organization conducted a poll of 1,030 male and female adults randomly selected across the nation. Whereas 94 percent of the respondents agreed that it is fairly important or very important to forgive, only 48 percent said they made it a practice to forgive others. In order to forgive a perpetrator, 83 percent responded, God's help is required. Only 15 percent said that they could forgive on their own.[3]

In essence, the poll suggests that almost all of us realize it is important to forgive. Even so, only half of us actually practice forgiveness. A small percentage of us believe we can forgive on our own. I wonder if those who think we can forgive on our own fall into the half of the respondents who practice forgiveness or the half who do not. I also wonder if those in the small number who claim to be self-sufficient have ever suffered grave injustices.

Perhaps the respondents failed to distinguish between *conditional* and *unconditional* forgiveness. *Unconditional* love and forgiveness lie beyond the reach of human beings. We are indeed capable of forgiving when the one who wounds us meets our demands of retribution. Our requirements, stated or not, usually demand remorse, repentance, apology, restitution, and a promise never to wrong us again. *Unconditional* forgiveness, however, is an altogether different matter. To forgive when there is no remorse in the perpetrator's heart, no apology, no repentance, and no assurance that things will be different in the future asks more of human beings than we are equipped to give. Moreover, forgiveness proves particularly difficult in the case of betrayal, injury to a child or spouse, or when the perpetrator derives a triumphant, demonic joy from his cruel deed. In short, *to forgive unconditionally requires help from God.*

The first Christian martyr following the death of Jesus was Stephen, a man full of the Holy Spirit. How else might his final words be explained as he lay dying under a bloody rain of stones? Praying as he breathed his last, Stephen whispered, "Lord, do not hold this sin against them!" (Acts 7:60 NIV). Likewise Hosea knew what it was like to suffer unjustly. His wife, Gomer, was an adulteress who boasted, "I will go after my lovers, who give me my bread and my water, my wool and my flax, my oil and my drink" (Hosea 2:5). As a result of her cavalier attitude, Gomer gave birth to a daughter and a son, neither of whom were fathered by Hosea. While enduring the humiliation of his wife's infidelity, the prophet heard the Lord say, "Go again, love a woman who is loved by her husband, yet an adulteress, even as the LORD loves the sons of Israel" (Hosea 3:1). In order to practice genuine love and unconditional forgiveness, Hosea needed an empowering word from God.

Difficult Questions

We encounter several questions when we speak of forgiving others. One common question is: *When I forgive do I have to forget?*

Some answer in the affirmative. "To forgive is to forget," they announce with all the assurance of a proud rooster announcing a new day. But I disagree. Of course we *may* forget when we forgive. However, the two should not be equated. If we have been hurt deeply enough, we may never forget the nauseating pain of that tortuous moment. Surely Christ has not forgotten his crucifixion. Yet even while on the cross, he cried, "Father, forgive them, for they know not what they do." When the trauma is unspeakable, there is no magical "delete" button to push.

Memory makes forgiveness possible. Philosophically speaking, we forgive precisely because we do remember.

Forgetting is not forgiving, but forgiving may lead to forgetting. An axiom of psychoanalysis warns us, "What cannot be remembered cannot be forgotten." I would add to that, "What cannot be remembered cannot be forgiven."

Martha Henry's son was killed in a drive-by shooting. Edward Henderson admitted to firing the fatal shot. While serving a life sentence in Indiana, Henderson discovered that he had a startling advocate for his release: Mrs. Henry! The forgiving mother appeared before the Indiana Clemency Board on Henderson's behalf seeking his parole. "I'm looking for him home by Christmas," she declared. Over the next fifteen years, she petitioned the board on four occasions for her son's killer. Henderson came to confess, "I hate to say this, but Mother Henry and I are closer than I am to my blood mother." Mrs. Henry will never forget the murder of her son, Calvin. But amazingly she has forgiven his killer.[4]

Another common question that surfaces when we consider forgiveness is: *Isn't avoiding the issue just as good as forgiving?* No, burying our head in the sand, pretending everything is fine is not the same as forgiveness, nor is it as healthy. Your blood pressure rises. Your acute anger becomes chronic. Your risk of heart disease increases. Your relationships are damaged. You may become depressed from anger turned inward. On the other hand, an honest facing of unacceptable behavior benefits both parties. Confrontation of wrong, as hard as it is, opens the door to forgiveness and healing.

David, nineteen, a minister's son, abused alcohol as a college student. When David got drunk, he grew violent. He soon developed a reputation for drinking heavily and fighting. His grades suffered. So did his relationships. His life reeled out of control. As he sat in my office and shared his story, I listened quietly. "I'm sure Dad knows," he related, "but he never says anything." "Maybe he doesn't know," I suggested. "No, he knows. He just thinks 'boys will be boys.' Pretends everything's cool." "What about your mother? Does she know?" "I didn't think so, 'til this past weekend. Boy, was I in for a surprise!" "What happened this past weekend?" I queried. "You won't believe it," he explained.

"I went home this past weekend, went out, got drunk with some of the guys, came stumblin' home about one in the morning. Tried to make sure I didn't make too much noise fallin' around and wake up my parents." "And?" I asked. "And when I was makin' it through the living room, I felt my leg rub up against something warm. Drunk as a skunk I looked down and there she was. Sitting in her rockin' chair with the light from the streetlight shining through the picture window right on her face, there sat Momma." "Uh-oh," I muttered. "There was Momma," he continued, "with tears runnin' down her face. Our eyes met. Momma never said a word. Just wept and shook. Just got up and went to her bed."

I wanted to ask a lot of questions. But David spoke again before I could get the words out. "Doc, I ain't drinkin' no more. I quit. I can't stand hurtin' Momma like that."

So no, I'd say avoiding a problem is not the same as forgiving. Before we can forgive, of course, we must first suffer a hurt. In our hurt, courageous, loving confrontation can open a door to transformation.

A third common question raised when considering forgiveness is: *How is forgiveness fair?* I take this to be a question of justice. What about judgment? To be sure forgiving is *not* suspending judgment. Forgiving is *not* pardoning, condoning, excusing, justifying, or ignoring the offense. To *pardon* is to release an offender from legal penalty; to *condone* is to overlook or accept an injustice; to *excuse* is to acknowledge legitimate reasons for wrongdoing; to *justify* is to decide that, in light of the circumstances, fault is not present; to *ignore* the injury is to pretend it never happened, which is a form of denial. Forgiveness is *none* of these things. *Forgiveness is judgment.* Blame lands squarely on the head of the criminal.

Although forgiveness gives us the freedom to let go of our resentment and desire for revenge, the challenge of justice is ever before us. God forgave Jimmy Lee Gray, but did not deliver him from prison. Jesus forgave the thief on the cross, but Jesus did not command angels to rescue the thief from the cross.

People can forgive; courts cannot. Justice and mercy differ. Never should we forgive and leave the situation unfair.

Sue, married and the mother of a young daughter, learned that she had a rare but fatal disease. According to doctors, Sue had less than a year to live. When her husband learned of his wife's terminal illness, he grew distant. Within months he filed for divorce, leaving his dying wife and young daughter all alone. A judge ordered child support payments to be made monthly. Several months passed. The father never made a payment. Since I served as interim pastor at Sue's church, she sought my counsel. "What should I do, forgive him?" she wondered.

What advice would you have given her? Should she forgive her husband and just let it go? "Yes, you should forgive him," I counseled. "But whatever you do, don't let him get away with not paying child support for your daughter."

Think about it. *Forgiveness* belongs in the realm of God; *justice* belongs in the realm of the law. Law and gospel differ. Society depends upon law and order. Citizens must obey rules. Individuals may choose to render rules breakable if they wish.

> No doubt, one of Christianity's major challenges is translating the virtues of love and forgiveness into a social order built upon justice.

Courts cannot. Without law, chaos breaks loose like a raging forest fire. No doubt, one of Christianity's major challenges is translating the virtues of love and forgiveness into a social order built upon justice, consistency, and stability. It is far too easy to confuse pardon and forgiveness. Pardon removes the offender from legal liability. Forgiveness has no such obligation. You may forgive a wrongdoer personally, while allowing the judicial system to run its course. Justice must prevail.

Forgiveness Redefined

Earlier I proposed a working definition of forgiveness: *Forgiveness is the removal of personal barriers within a relationship caused by wrongdoing, real or imagined.* Let's now expand the definition. The forgiveness coin has two sides: One side results from a violation of fairness; the other side stems from a response of bitterness and a burning desire to strike back. In other words relational barriers are erected due to

> *Forgiveness is the removal of personal barriers within a relationship caused by wrongdoing, real or imagined, on the one hand, **and** resentment and a desire for revenge, on the other.*

harm done to us, *combined with* a harmful response *from* us. Therefore our unabridged definition of forgiveness reads as follows: *Forgiveness is the removal of personal barriers within a relationship caused by wrongdoing, real or imagined, on the one hand, **and** resentment and a desire for revenge, on the other.*

Resentment *must* be present in order to forgive or there is nothing to forgive. Forgiveness calls for letting go of the resentment and the wish for revenge. When you have been wronged and the need to forgive is absent, either damage insufficient to merit a crisis occurred, or reaction to the offense never progressed beyond anger.

Examples for Reflection

When you are struck by a crisis of forgiveness, repentance by the offending party isn't necessary for you to grant forgiveness. Otherwise you, the victim, might become a slave to rage forever. For example, in the Old Testament we read about Joseph who was only seventeen when his father, who loved him dearly, presented him with a coat of many colors. Joseph's brothers, seeing how their father adored their younger sibling, hated Joseph. With intense envy, they plotted to kill Joseph. Seizing the unsuspecting young man, the brothers threw him into a pit in the wilderness to die. Soon a trade caravan approached, and they decided to sell Joseph into slavery instead of leaving him to die.

After eventually landing in Egypt, Joseph rose to heights of power, ruling with authority surpassed only by Pharaoh. Many years later, famine ravaged the land of Canaan, and Joseph's brothers found themselves standing before him seeking food. They did not recognize the powerful figure as their younger brother, although Joseph knew them immediately. Would he seek revenge? Hadn't his brothers tried to murder him? Didn't they tear him away from his father and sell him as a slave? Later, during the climactic encounter with his brothers, Joseph wept loudly and blurted, "I am Joseph! Is my father still alive? . . . I am your brother Joseph, whom you sold into Egypt. Now do not be grieved or angry with yourselves, because you sold me here, for God sent me before you to preserve life" (Gen. 45:3–5). The brothers surely froze in absolute shock and fear!

The incredible story of Joseph's love and forgiveness continued with a moving reunion of the family. Joseph "kissed all his brothers and wept on them, and afterward his brothers talked with him" (Gen. 45:15). Soon the reunion of Joseph and Israel, his father, witnessed a river of tears as well as great rejoicing. When their father died, however, the brothers grew afraid. "What if Joseph bears a grudge against us and pays us back in full for all the wrong which we did to him!" (Gen. 50:15). Instead Joseph consoled his brothers, saying, "Do not be afraid, for am I in God's place? As for you, you meant evil against me, but God meant it for good. . . . So therefore, do not be afraid; I will provide for you and your little ones" (Gen. 50:19–21). The story concludes by noting that Joseph "comforted them and spoke kindly to them" (Gen. 50:21).

Joseph found the love and strength to forgive his brothers because he was capable of viewing the events of his life through God's eyes. His choice, after all, was fairly straightforward: become bitter or become better. By inviting God into his crisis, Joseph chose wisely. Joseph's inspiring character remains legendary. His power to forgive came directly from God.

Forgiveness isn't always so beautifully given. In the Gospel of Luke, Jesus told the parable of a wasteful son, an unforgiving brother, and a loving father. The young, irresponsible son leaves home, wastes his inheritance in wild living, then returns home tired, broken, and worse for the wear. Upon seeing his son, the boy's father runs to meet him, embraces his son, kisses him, and calls for a celebration. The older son becomes angry and refuses to join the lavish party. Complaining bitterly to his father, he screams, "You have never given me a young goat, so that I might celebrate with my friends; but when this son of yours came, who has devoured your wealth with prostitutes, you killed the fattened calf for him" (Luke 15:29–30). At the conclusion of the story, the older son has forgiven neither his brother nor his father.

When we forgive our attitude changes. Change of attitude leads to change of behavior. The elder brother in Jesus's parable refused to forgive his younger brother. He also refused to forgive his father's conduct. In ugly fashion, his attitude and actions correlate. Mean thoughts and bitter attitudes serve as seeds to produce a harvest of hateful deeds. If ever there was a saying that reminds us how ideas have consequences, it is this one:

Sow a thought, reap a deed;
sow a deed, reap a habit;
sow a habit, reap a character;
sow a character, reap a destiny.

Where we spend our eternal destiny can usually be traced back to our thought life. There, in our innermost being, we accept or reject God in our life, thereby sealing our destiny. Self-centeredness, which prevented the older son from being reconciled to his younger brother, prevented reconciliation with his father as well. In the story, the father represents God. By rejecting his father's attitude of reconciliation, the older son was powerless to forgive his brother. When we are right with God, we can forgive and will forgive. When we reject God, any hope of receiving or practicing unconditional forgiveness vanishes.

In order to forgive we must refuse to demonize our adversary. Each of us is loved by God and created in God's image. Still we are each capable of good and evil. The noted German poet and novelist Goethe confessed that he had never known of a crime he might be incapable of committing. "If only it were all so simple!" added Alexander Solzhenitsyn, a former political prisoner of the Communist Soviet Union. "If only there were evil people . . . and it were necessary only to separate them from the rest of us and destroy them. But," he sighed, "the line dividing good and evil cuts through the heart of every human being."[5]

> *Each of us is loved by God and created in God's image. Still we are each capable of good and evil.*

The older brother in Jesus's parable wanted power. Holding a white-knuckled grip on resentment, he sought to punish his offending brother and forgiving father. They would pay. Wielding the power of bitterness like a blunt instrument, he hit with the intent to harm. Love, so clearly present in the father, was missing in the older boy's heart. The love of power versus the power of love contrast sharply in the story. "Where love rules there is no will to power," Carl Jung wrote, "and where power predominates, there love is lacking." Forgiveness springs from love. However, where love is absent, forgiveness is impossible.[6]

Could there ever come a time or occasion when forgiveness should be denied? In Simon Wiesenthal's haunting book *The Sunflower*, the author, a survivor of the holocaust, tells the story of a young Jew who was taken from a concentration camp to hear the deathbed confession of a Nazi soldier. The soldier, an SS trooper, was haunted horribly by memories of a mass murder in which he had participated. Jewish men, women, and children, perhaps as many as two hundred, had been herded into a house. The doors had been locked. Machine guns had been trained on the exits. The house was set ablaze. Any who tried to escape had been riddled with bullets. Hand grenades had been thrown through the windows. A man clutching a small child had jumped from a second story window. The Nazi, who now lay dying, had fired mercilessly. A child with black hair and dark eyes haunted him. "I cannot die . . . without coming clean," the soldier confessed. "I . . . I am left here with my guilt. . . . I want to die in peace." He whispered, "I have longed to talk to a Jew and beg forgiveness from him. . . . I know that what I am asking is almost too much for you, but without your answer I cannot die in peace."[7]

What would you have done? Did the young Jew have the responsibility of extending forgiveness to the confessing murderer? Would you have granted or denied forgiveness to the dying man? Silence filled the room of the dying soldier. Then, the young Jew related, "At last I made up my mind and without a word I left the room."

Responses That Fall Short of Forgiveness

Whenever we suffer an injustice, *retribution* and *forgiveness* rush to offer themselves as two opposing responses from which we may choose. Of course we may also choose to ignore the wrong. Reasons for electing to ignore a wrong may include love, retribution, fear, poor coping capabilities, or inadequate conflict management skills. In addition to ignoring a cruelty, pardoning, condoning, excusing, justifying, and forgetting are all possible reactions to violations of our persons. Some of these responses may be motivated by love, others by a sense of fairness, and still others by denial, or for some unfathomable reason. As explained previously, none of these options constitute forgiveness. In order for forgiveness to occur, *guilt must be established.* Judgment must fall. Excuses are unacceptable. Sure, every deed has a cause. But cause doesn't remove responsibility. There is always a story, but not all stories excuse. "I did what I did because . . ."; "I didn't mean to do it"; "I couldn't help it"; "I was only following orders." All of these approaches hope to dismiss judgment. Reasons and excuses differ. The former hold water; the latter do not.

Good friends of mine lost their teenage son in an automobile accident involving alcohol and speeding on the part of another person. For the guilty driver of the car to say, "I didn't mean to do it," could never alter the fact that the accident was his fault. It is true that the death of our friends' son followed what is sometimes referred to as the Law of Unintended Consequences. The inebriated driver surely did not intend to cause the death of an innocent person. Nevertheless, drunk driving is illegal, foolhardy, and merits strong judgment. Excuses fail, leaving in their wake a crisis of forgiveness.

The Healthy Process

Any time we suffer injury at the hands of a wrongdoer, we grieve. Grief and loss almost always go hand in hand. As victims, we suffer loss of self-esteem, loss of dignity, loss of possessions, loss of health, loss of a dream, loss of loved ones, and loss of well-being. Therefore we must work through the stages of grief to regain emotional equilibrium. Elisabeth Kübler-Ross identifies the stages of grief as *denial* or *shock, anger, bargaining, depression,* and finally *acceptance.*[8] The process of working toward forgiveness should not be rushed. Anger, for example, is a justifiable response to unfairness. Venting anger may prove to be therapeutic. Suppressing anger, on the other hand, may cause problems later.

Violations of fairness need to be addressed honestly. Feelings should not be suppressed. Premature forgiveness poses a temptation to avoid. Forgiveness is a choice, but it is also a process. The process leads, when the time is right, to the removal of barriers within a relationship. Resentment is exchanged for goodwill. Sometimes, however, we think we have forgiven when we have not. When a remembered wound to our ego causes hostilities to resurface, the injury has not been forgiven.

David replaced Saul as king of Israel. Years later, Shimei, a man from the house of Saul, cursed David publicly, threw stones at him, and shouted, "Get out, get out, you man of bloodshed, and worthless fellow! . . . You are taken in your own evil, for you are a man of bloodshed!" (2 Sam. 16:7–8). Abishai, one of the king's servants, begged David, "Why should this dead dog curse my lord the king? Let me go over now and cut off his head" (2 Sam. 16:9). But David replied, "If he curses, and if the LORD has told him, 'Curse David,' then who shall say, 'Why have you done so?' . . . Let him alone and let him curse . . . Perhaps the LORD will look on my affliction and return good to me instead of his cursing this day" (2 Sam. 16:10–12).

David was portrayed in the Bible as a paragon of virtue, projecting humility, graciousness, patience, understanding, and forgiveness. Some time later, Shimei came to his senses, fell down before the king, and pleaded for forgiveness. "Let not my lord consider me guilty, nor remember what your servant did wrong on the day when my lord the king came out from Jerusalem, so that the king would take it to heart. For your servant knows that I have sinned" (2 Sam. 19:19–20). Again Abishai blurted, "Should not Shimei be put to death for this, because he cursed the LORD's anointed?" (2 Sam. 19:21). As before, David rebuked Abishai, then said to Shimei, "You shall not die."

Years later as David lay dying in old age, he charged Solomon his son, who was succeeding him as king, "I am going the way of all the earth. Be strong, therefore, and show yourself a man. Keep the charge of the LORD your God, to walk in His ways, to keep His statutes, His commandments, His ordinances, and His testimonies . . ." (1 Kings 2:2–3). David then reminded Solomon of God's promise, "If your sons are careful of their way, to walk before Me in truth with all their heart and with all their soul, you shall not lack a man on the throne of Israel" (1 Kings 2:4). David appeared to be an exemplar of spirituality. What happened next shocks us!

"Behold, there is with you Shimei. . . . now it was he who cursed me with a violent curse on the day I went to Mahanaim," David breathed to Solomon. "But when he came down to me at the Jordan, I swore to him by the LORD, saying, 'I will not put you to death with the sword.' Now therefore," David insisted, "do not let him go unpunished, for you are a wise man; and you will know what you ought to do to him, and you will bring his gray hair down to Sheol with blood" (1 Kings 2:8–9). Following David's death, Solomon honored his father's deathbed request by executing Shimei. Before his execution, the allegedly forgiven man heard these words, "You know all the evil . . . which you did to my father

David; therefore the LORD shall return your evil on your own head" (1 Kings 2:44). So Shimei died.

So much for David's legacy as a model of forgiveness. We must admit that it is true that David passionately sought God's forgiveness following his adultery with Bathsheba and his subsequent successful plot to have her husband killed. In fact, Psalm 51, attributed to David during those days, remains the prince of penitential psalms. So what went wrong in the case of Shimei? If David could swallow his pride and seek forgiveness from God, why could he not grant forgiveness to Shimei?

First, we must admit we do not know the entire story. We know only what we know. Based on what we read, however, David may not have allowed a healthy process of grief to run its course. By that I mean his earlier alleged forgiveness may have been premature. David never gave expression to any feelings of hurt, humiliation, or hostility toward Shimei. Rather he apparently suppressed his true feelings. Anger, shame, and resentment never surfaced, even though he was cursed viciously and pelted with stones. He never addressed Shimei regarding the injustice of his attack. David pressed no charges. He levied no penalty. He made no move to insure his protection against a future attack. He treated the matter far too lightly it seems. An injustice politely ushered out the back door during the daylight often returns in the night to

> *Cheap forgiveness brings expensive bills.*

kick down the front door. *Cheap forgiveness brings expensive bills.* David paid far too much for his show of cheap grace. As for poor Shimei, cheap grace cost him his life.

As David's deathbed words revealed, he harbored intense anger over Shimei's violation of him. However, David never confronted Shimei about the matter. Furthermore, when Shimei approached him, David declined the opportunity for honest dialogue. Nor did he, as far as we know, verbalize his rage to God, or anyone else. Left undressed, the open wound festered. By refusing to forgive, David forfeited peace of mind, peace with others (with Shimei, but also Joab, whose execution he ordered as well), and peace with God. Perhaps David was depressed. Unresolved conflict and anger turned inward invite depression. Like any of us who has ever had a crisis of forgiveness, David needed God's help.

> *In prayer, as with all of life,*
> *honesty is the best policy.*

God's Finest Example

One of my professors in seminary called attention to our flawed pattern of problem solving. "When we find ourselves stressed to the edge of our limits," he said, "our first line of defense is to try to handle the crisis ourselves. When that fails," he noted, "we turn to others for help. When relief still does not come," the professor observed, "as a last resort, we cry out to God for help. Wouldn't it be good," he lamented, "if we reversed the order?"

In prayer, as with all of life, honesty is the best policy. An honest prayer may begin, "Lord, help me to *want* to forgive, because right now, I don't even want to!" Maybe if the Lord can first change our hearts so that we *want* to forgive, he can then lead us to take the next step and the next, until we *have* forgiven.

God is love. Therefore *love is the unifying principle of the created order.* Violations of love plunge creation into chaos. Order becomes disorder. Orientation collapses into disorientation, which in turn cries out for reorientation. Only love, unselfish love, *agape* love, gives birth to forgiveness. Only forgiveness can remove barriers within a relationship caused by wrongdoing. Only forgiveness can rid our souls of resentment. Only forgiveness can save us from the poison of revenge. Why forgive? Because nothing else works.

The single most powerful illustration of love and forgiveness I am familiar with comes from Jesus on the cross. I am totally disarmed by this loving act. While we were *killing* him, he loved us and forgave us! Surely he *must* have been tempted to want to "get us back"! To be sure, Jesus was no milquetoast Christ. He had expressed his feelings strongly and honestly all along the way to the cross. To the high priest who questioned him cynically, he replied, "Why do you question Me? Question those who have heard what I spoke to them; they know what I said" (John 18:21). To the Roman officer who struck him for speaking defiantly to the high priest, he demanded, "If I have spoken wrongly, testify of the wrong; but if rightly, why do you strike Me?" (John 18:23). To Pilate who jeered, "Do You not know that I have authority to release You, and I have authority to crucify You?" he rebutted, "You would have no authority over Me, unless it had been given you from above" (John 19:10–11). Even to God, whom he felt had deserted him, he cried, "'*Eli, Eli,*

> The true miracle is that I want to love others the way I am loved. Christ is contagious.

lama sabachthani?' that is, "My God, My God, why have You forsaken Me?" (Matt. 27:46).

Yet, his grace is impossible to miss, and for me, impossible to resist. "Father, forgive them; for they do not know what they are doing" prayed the crucified one (Luke 23:34). I don't know what to do with that amazing grace. Except melt. We were *killing* him, and he loved us and forgave us! He sees me at my worst but loves me anyway. That changes me. I not only repent of my evil ways, but I accept myself, dark side and all, knowing that my worst has been exposed, and still I am loved. The true miracle is that I want to love others the way I am loved. Christ is contagious.

"A new commandment I give to you, that you love one another, even as I have loved you, that you also love one another," Jesus said (John 13:34). Such love empowers forgiveness for others. When, in our humanness, we are tempted to turn our backs on love and forgiveness, there is a place we can go for help. That place is a person.

> For we do not have a high priest who cannot sympathize with our weaknesses, but One who has been tempted in all things as we are, yet without sin. Therefore let us draw near with confidence to the throne of grace, so that we may receive mercy and find grace to help in time of need.
>
> Hebrews 4:15–16

Lord Jesus, help us to forgive others as you forgive us. Amen.

Forgiveness for Self

As hard as it may be to forgive others, the more daunting task sometimes is forgiving ourselves. As much as we hate to admit it, we aren't perfect. We all mess up. No matter how much we love each other, we *still* hurt each other. We still fall short of all that God commands. Socrates asked, "How is it that men know what is good, but do what is bad?" Even a writer of Scripture like the apostle Paul confessed, "The good that I want, I do not do, but I practice the very evil that I do not want" (Rom. 7:19).

In addition to hurting others, we commit secret sins that hurt ourselves as well. Our inner voice says, "No! Don't do it. You know better!" But we ignore the internal parent. We are adults now; we can do as we please. A competing voice hisses, "Go ahead. It's okay. Who will know?" Nothing new here. Same old story. Same sad results. "Gotcha!" laughs the tempter! Adam's apple gets lodged in our throats. Death begins. We need saving. Only a forgiveness maneuver will work.

Because we know we are not perfect, each of us lives with a sense of self-rejection. No one sees himself as completely whole. We wrestle with our guilt; we struggle with our shame. Guilt says, "I did a bad thing." Shame says, "I am a bad person!" The distinction between guilt and shame is critical. Since self as subject judges self as object, our pain is compounded. Sometimes, however, both our guilt and shame need absolution. We have all violated our consciences, and we pay dearly for those violations.

Some time ago, my family was served by a young mailman who was extraordinarily courteous and friendly. His route brought him to our home late each day as I arrived home from work. "Good day, Reverend." "How are you today, Reverend?" "Please give my best to the missus and the little ones, Reverend." "Have a nice evening, Reverend." Always Reverend. Always the sincerest respect for my calling as a minister.

How many times did he find tired feet, drooping spirits, and sagging shoulders at the end of my driveway only to leave "the Reverend" smiling again, spirits buoyed, steps quickened along the short walk to the family door, mail securely in hand?

What were *his* spirits like? How was *his* day going? Who was *he*? Who knows? I never asked. Not *one* question did I ever ask him! He was just a mailman, wasn't he? Why bother? Why should I care what his life was like? So many questions I never asked. So many words I never spoke. So many opportunities I never took. "Is it nothing to all you who pass this way? Look and see if there is any pain like my pain," the writer of the book of Lamentations cried (Lam. 1:12). "Most men live lives of quiet desperation," wrote Henry David Thoreau. So my twenty-eight-year-old mailman, husband of only two years, and a friend of mine (who never heard me say it nor ever saw me show it) chose to end his life of quiet desperation, in suicide.

How can I ever forgive myself? Some Reverend! I didn't even know his name.

Edwin Arlington Robinson's poem "Richard Cory" haunts me whenever I think about my inconsideration of my mailman.

> Whenever Richard Cory went down town,
> We people on the pavement looked at him:
> He was a gentleman from sole to crown,
> Clean favored, and imperially slim.
>
> And he was always quietly arrayed,
> And he was always human when he talked;
> But still he fluttered pulses when he said,
> "Good-morning," and he glittered when he walked.
>
> And he was rich—yes, richer than a king—
> And admirably schooled in every grace:
> In fine, we thought that he was everything
> To make us wish that we were in his place.
>
> So on we worked, and waited for the light,
> And went without the meat, and cursed the bread;
> And Richard Cory, one calm summer night,
> Went home and put a bullet through his head.[1]

"Randall," a friend of mine said, "let me tell you about Charlie." "Sure," I said. So he began. "Charlie's dead now. Died a few years back. Old. Broken. Tired. Drunk mostly. Every day of Charlie's life, he bought a newspaper. First thing, every morning. Carried it in his back pocket all day long. Had a nice pen and pencil set he carried in his front pocket. Everywhere he went he carried that newspaper and pen and pencil set. But Randall, Charlie couldn't read or write. First thing every morning, long as I can remember, from the time he was a young man 'til the time he died, Charlie carried that newspaper in his back pocket and that pen and pencil set in his front pocket. But Charlie couldn't read or write a word."

163

Is this a description of us or what? We're all Charlie, aren't we? And some of us are Richard Cory! To what extreme do we go to hide our pain? To what extent do we go to conceal our inadequacies, our hurts, our needs? And God forbid, just where does that road lead?

Our pretty masks are not pretty. We live, and sometimes we die, in our guilt and our shame, behind our masks. We cannot forgive ourselves. Forgiveness of ourself is too hard. To suffer silently is easier. Or maybe, even to die. Somehow we must remove that ball and chain.

A certain man went for a walk in the forest. As the sun went down and darkness began to fall, the hiker thought, *I'd better be finding my way home now. Soon darkness will engulf the woods, and I will become hopelessly lost.* So the man tried first one path in hope, then a second in anxiety, and finally a third in fear. But alas, none of the paths led out of the forest. Desperately searching late into the night for a way out of the forest, the weary and frightened pilgrim at last stumbled upon another man. "Thank goodness," the lost soul cried, "another human being! Look, I'm lost. Can you show me the way out of the forest?" "No. I can't," the second man said. "I'm lost too. But maybe we can help each other. Maybe we can share with each other the paths that we have tried that have disappointed us. Then together perhaps we can find the way out."

Nothing is more frightening, or dangerous, than to find ourselves lost in the deep darkness of guilt and shame. Alas, no path proves more elusive than the path to self-forgiveness. Our desperate search for the holy trail seems all the more hopeless when we go it alone. On the other hand, our quest never holds more promise than when we travel in community. Together perhaps we can find our way out of the darkness of despair into the light of love and self-forgiveness.

Hope

We all make choices about who we want to be. To become who we are not, we must first accept who we are. We accept ourselves by owning and telling our life story. Do we see ourselves as victim, pilgrim, learner, hero, or villain? To see ourselves as villain poses, perhaps, the greatest challenge. Owning our part in the mess in which we find ourselves requires maturation and introspection. However, the greatest challenge of all is granting ourselves grace, forgiveness, and new beginnings.

> We accept ourselves by owning
> and telling our life story.

When we are able to accept our imperfections and deal with them in a healthy manner, we are able to live under a canopy of goodness, love, joy, and peace.

As a Russian with title and nobility, Leo Tolstoy, author of *War and Peace*, one of the most acclaimed novels of all time, wrestled with his exalted station in life in the face of poverty and suffering all around. Choosing to surrender his life of privilege for a radical Christian life lived out among his countrymen, he said, "Everybody thinks of changing the world; nobody thinks of changing himself."[2] Gandhi, who sought to insure right treatment of all people in India and South Africa, encouraged, "Be the change in the world you want to see."[3]

The first step in deliberate change involves recognizing the need for it. Put differently, the first step in problem solving lies in admitting the problem. When the change we desire is self-forgiveness, or the problem we wish to solve is self-rejection, our first move is to *name* the issue.

In his nationwide best seller *People of the Lie*, Scott Peck wrote, "It is not their sins per se that characterize evil people, rather it is the subtlety and persistence and consistency of their sins. This is because the central defect of the evil is not the sin but the refusal to acknowledge it."[4] In *The Road Less Traveled*, Peck wrote, "Evil people hate the light because it reveals themselves to themselves."[5]

Denial is not a river in Egypt. Denial is a deadly malady. Guilty secrets eat away at our souls and our sanity. When at last we are ready to treat the disease of denial with the medicine of truth, wellness awaits.

Our need for wellness and self-forgiveness may stem from addictive and compulsive disorders. Alcoholism, drug abuse, power addictions, emotional, verbal, and physical abuse, sexual

> *Denial is not a river in Egypt.*
> *Denial is a deadly malady.*

abuse, chemical, emotional, and violence co-dependency are all major problems, which can be solved when acknowledged. Others include eating disorders, sexual addiction, and work addiction. Guilt and shame are legitimate feelings when we hurt ourselves or others as a result of one or more of these disorders. When our coping abilities finally fail, when our pain is more than we can stand, when we are ready for self-honesty, help is available.

The second step toward change is taking action. While there are many reasons we need to forgive ourselves, certainly addictive behaviors have caused immense damage to many people. Countless numbers of persons have been helped by twelve step programs. Following are the twelve steps most organizations use.

1. We admitted we were powerless over (alcoholism, drugs, other people, a compulsive disorder), and our lives had become unmanageable.
2. We came to believe that a Power greater than ourselves could restore us to sanity.

3. We made a decision to turn our will and our life over to the care of God as we understand God.
4. We made a searching and fearless moral inventory of ourselves.
5. We admitted to God, to ourselves, and to another human being the exact nature of our wrongs.
6. We became entirely willing to have God remove all these defects of character.
7. We humbly asked God to remove our shortcomings.
8. We made a list of all persons we have harmed and became willing to make amends to them all.
9. We made direct amends to such people wherever possible, except when to do so would injure them or others.
10. We continue to take personal inventory, and when we are wrong, promptly admit it.
11. We seek through prayer and meditation to improve our conscious contact with God as we understand God, praying only for knowledge of God's will for us and power to carry that out.
12. Having had a spiritual awakening as a result of these steps, we try to carry this message to others and to practice these principles in all of our affairs.[6]

These twelve steps have enabled thousands, maybe millions, to change destructive behavior patterns. These same steps may very well rescue us from self-destruction as well.

For those longing for true forgiveness, however, the twelve step program contains a glaring omission. Missing altogether is any direct mention of *forgiveness* from God, significant others, or *self*. To be sure, changed behavior equals changed lives, not only for an addict or abuser, but for an entire family. For that we give thanks. The future shines brightly whenever a prisoner of the present escapes the dungeon of addiction. But what about the haunting past? What about the need to *be* forgiven and *to forgive ourselves* for all the wrong we have done, all the people we have hurt, and all the consequences that remain?

Recognizing our helplessness, turning our lives over to God, admitting our wrongdoing, making restitution, and prayer are all-powerful, life-changing measures. These moves may even lead to self-forgiveness. Certainly when we consider that all sin is, at heart, separation from God, others, nature, and self, the twelve step program does indeed *indirectly* effect a fragile forgiveness with God, others, and self, as barriers to oneness collapse. Is it possible, however, to find a way to somehow upgrade forgiveness from indirect to direct, from fragile to firm?

What do we do when the wash is done but a stubborn stain remains? What might we do with a sin that seems impossible to wash from our memory? What do we do when general forgiveness clothes us, but the lack of self-forgiveness in one tortuous area makes us feel naked and ashamed?

Justification

Steve loved his wife, son, and daughter. Theirs was a home where prayer and church attendance was routine. So was Steve's drinking. Steve had been an honorable mention all-American athlete in college. His teammates seemed to be able to go out for beers without alcohol taking control of their lives. Not Steve. He drank long; he drank often. After marrying his wife, Susan, his drinking problem worsened. By the time the children came along, Steve was drinking early and late. As the babies grew into childhood, Steve would often disappear for days at a time. Susan and Steve fought. Tears flowed. The family became dysfunctional as "the secret" was kept from the grandparents and others.

Steve related to me a time when he sat reading the sports page in his easy chair at home as little Stephanie jumped into his lap, hugged his neck, and begged, "Daddy, please don't go out drinking tonight. Puh-lease, Daddy. I love you. Please don't go, Daddy. Promise?"

Steve softly wept as he shared this painful memory. "Doc, I knew as she hugged my neck and begged me that I would go out anyway." Susan and Steve eventually divorced. "I've made a mess of my life," he sobbed. "But the *one* thing I can't forgive myself for is what I've done to Stephanie, how I hurt her."

How can Steve ever forgive himself? *First,* Steve must receive God's forgiveness. Then, but not before, he will be able to forgive himself. *Without God's forgiveness, we may only attain a false peace, if any at all.* Ours is a longing to remove the curse of estrangement from God, nature, family, others, and our true selves, due to our heinous sins. Restoring oneness, harmony, and peace to our lives will constitute a long-awaited blessing. That sometimes elusive blessing is forgiveness.

Paul Tournier observes in *Guilt and Grace* that there are two solutions for the problem of guilt, one false, the other true. In the false category, he places both moral effort and atoning sacrifices or ritual. The only true solution to the problem of guilt, he argues, is atonement of our sins by God himself.[7]

I think that Tournier is right. According to Christian theology, the world was founded upon grace. Who among us would argue that we deserve life or forgiveness? What

> *We all fail. Our souls are famished;*
> *let us cease to gnaw the stale crust*
> *of "moral perfection,"*
> *when grace sets a feast before us.*

have we done to deserve life? Forgiveness of wrong, by its very nature, cannot be deserved. To be sure, justice is a moral absolute. Yet only grace works in forgiveness. Were we to plead for justice, all our injustices would merit punishment. Forgiveness then always springs from grace. By grace God forgives us, and by grace God empowers us to forgive ourselves and others.

Moral effort is certainly commendable. Moral effort, however, can neither yield perfection nor atone for imperfection. We all fail. Our souls are famished; let us cease to gnaw the stale crust of "moral perfection," when grace sets a feast before us.

Should our hopes for holistic forgiveness rest instead with ritual? The ancient Hebrews celebrated a Day of Atonement in which sins were covered (Leviticus 16). In this ceremony two goats were chosen to bear the sins of Israel. One goat was slain as a sin offering to the Lord. The second goat became a scapegoat:

> Then Aaron shall lay both of his hands on the head of the live goat, and confess over it all the iniquities of the sons of Israel and all their transgressions in regard to all their sins; and he shall lay them on the head of the goat and send it away into the wilderness. . . . The goat shall bear on itself all their iniquities.
>
> Leviticus 16:21–22

The first goat was for the Lord; the second one was for Azazel (Lev. 16:8). The Hebrew term *azazel* is generally interpreted as "scapegoat" in various translations. However, the term may refer to a desert demon. (Elsewhere Azazel is identified as the leader of fallen angels who are sentenced to life beneath rocks in the desert as they await judgment.)

What is significant about these atoning sacrifices is the removal of sin from humans. The roles of the two goats remind us that sin is deadly, and that evil must go somewhere. The first animal died in place of the sinful people; the second one returned evil to the demons, or "devil." Soon, however, the false security of Israel's ritual was shattered by the psalmist

and prophets, who insisted that God desired right relationships, not religious rites:

> You do not delight in sacrifice, otherwise I would give it;
>> You are not pleased with burnt offering.
> The sacrifices of God are a broken spirit;
>> a broken and a contrite heart, O God, You will not despise.
>
> Psalm 51:16–17

> "What are your multiplied sacrifices to Me?"
>> says the LORD. . . .
>> "I take no pleasure in the blood of bulls, lambs or goats. . . .
> Bring your worthless offerings no longer . . ."
>
> Isaiah 1:11, 13

> Even though you offer up to Me burnt offerings and your
>> grain offerings,
>> I will not accept them. . . .
> But let justice roll down like waters
>> and righteousness like an ever-flowing stream.
>
> Amos 5:22, 24

> For I delight in loyalty rather than sacrifice,
>> and in the knowledge of God rather than burnt offerings.
>
> Hosea 6:6

> With what shall I come to the LORD
>> and bow myself before the God on high?
>> Shall I come to Him with burnt offerings,
>> with yearling calves?
> Does the LORD take delight in thousands of rams? . . .
> He has told you, O man, what is good;
>> and what does the LORD require of you
>> but to do justice, to love kindness,
>> and to walk humbly with your God?
>
> Micah 6:6, 8

171

I did not speak to your fathers, or command them in the day that
I brought them out of the land of Egypt, concerning burnt offer-
ings and sacrifices. But this is what I commanded them, saying,
"Obey My voice, and I will be your God, and you will be My
people; and you will walk in all the way which I command you,
that it may be well with you."

Jeremiah 7:22–23

We are all in this forgiveness predicament together. We
all sin, and every sin must be paid for. All sinners need to
be justified. "For all have sinned and fall short of the glory
of God, being justified as a gift by His grace through the
redemption which is in Christ Jesus" (Rom. 3:23–24). The
good news is that "God demonstrates His own love toward us,
in that while we were yet sinners, Christ died for us" (Rom.
5:8). We should think of "justified" as "just-as-if-I'd" never
sinned, encouraged Dallas Willard in *The Divine Conspiracy*.[8]

> *We are all in this forgiveness predicament together.*

The Lord says, "I, even I, am the one who wipes out your
transgressions for My own sake, and I will not remember
your sins" (Isa. 43:25). "God pardons like a mother," said
Henry Ward Beecher, nineteenth-century American clergyman and abolitionist, "who kisses the offense into everlasting
forgetfulness." When God forgives our sins, that is when we
are justified. God does not remember our sins. It is "just-as-
if-I'd" never sinned.

As Tournier asserted, the only true solution to our problem of guilt is atonement through God himself. "*At-one-
ment*" with God, others, and self comes not through priests
standing "daily ministering and offering time after time the
same sacrifices, which can never take away sins. . . . [rather]
by one offering He [Jesus] has perfected for all time those
who are sanctified. . . . 'and their sins and their lawless deeds

I will remember no more.' Now where there is forgiveness of these things, there is no longer any offering for sin" (Heb. 10:11, 14, 17–18).

We have a difficult time accepting forgiveness of our sins and forgiving ourselves as well, don't we? Why? Because we believe our sins must be *paid* for. When Jesus died on the cross for the forgiveness of our sins, *God* paid. A divine idea! Forgiveness, however, is not an idea; forgiveness is a person. Jesus forgives.

Grace

"We do not come to grace; grace comes to us," observes Scott Peck in *The Road Less Traveled*.[9] Isn't this what John meant when he proclaimed,

> In the beginning was the Word, and the Word was with God, and the Word was God. . . . And the Word became flesh, and dwelt among us . . . full of grace and truth. . . . For of His fullness we have all received, and grace upon grace. For the Law was given through Moses; grace and truth were realized through Jesus Christ.
>
> John 1:1, 14, 16–17

What is grace? Grace is a river. Wherever its course winds, souls blossom like flowers. The river flows here. There. By

> *Forgiveness is not an idea;*
> *forgiveness is a person.*
> *Jesus forgives.*

me. By you. By all of us. We swim in it. Float down it. Drink its cool waters. From where does the river flow? From the altar of God, Ezekiel said. From the cross, Jesus said. "I am the Living Water," said the Christ. Thirsty? Drink! The stream exists for you. For me. For us. "Come to the waters and drink freely," invites Isaiah. "Drink and never thirst," offers the Christ. "Drink!"

The church has been showering living water upon parched souls for twenty-one centuries. *Grace means that there is nothing I can ever do to make God love me more, and nothing I can ever do to make God love me less.* Grace is rooted in God's character not mine. I am not always good, but God always loves me. Grace always feels out of place, kind of like a moustache on grandmother. Sin is like sand on the retina. It is like chewing tinfoil. Sin is to the memory as wrinkles are to cardboard:

> *Grace means that there is nothing I can ever do to make God love me more, and nothing I can ever do to make God love me less.*

impossible to remove! Grace on us is like water on wax: It has a hard time soaking in. Nevertheless grace offers unconditional love and forgiveness. God *is* grace! With two thousand years of sweet grace served, guilt-ridden sinners should be drawn to the church like kittens to warm milk. But is this always so?

In *What's So Amazing about Grace?* Philip Yancey shares the following story he heard from a friend who works with the destitute in Chicago.

A prostitute came to me in wretched straits, homeless, sick, unable to buy food for her two-year-old daughter. Through sobs and tears, she told me she had been renting out her daughter—two years old!—to men interested in kinky sex. She made more renting out her daughter for an hour than she could earn on her own in a night. She had to do it, she said, to support her own drug habit. I could hardly bear hearing her sordid story. For one thing, it made me legally liable—I'm required to report cases of child abuse. I had no idea what to say to this woman. At last I asked if she had ever thought of going to a church for help. I will never forget the look of pure, naïve shock that crossed her face. "Church!" she cried. "Why would I ever go there? I was already feeling terrible about myself. They'd just make me feel worse."[10]

Perhaps author William Miller was right when he said, "Too much morality is as bad as too little morality."[11] If Miller's statement is true, the church *and* the prostitute fall under the same judgment. Like the elder and younger brothers in the parable of the prodigal son, one acknowledges his sin; the other is as blind as a bat. Hadn't the prostitute already judged herself? How could she ever forgive herself? What she needed was grace. And then, of course, help.

Years ago when my daughter Alyson Elise was a young child, I was going overboard in correcting her for something I felt she had done wrong. She listened contritely and respectfully. As I went on and on, she at last said, "Daddy, God and I are not twins!" Alyson Elise had accepted her judgment, granted herself grace, and had become my teacher. There is a time for judgment and a time for grace.

One cold winter's day when our daughter Shannon was four, maybe five years old, she found me trying to get a fire going in the fireplace and hit me from behind with a question. "Daddy, you're a doctor, right?" Continuing to stoke the fire I answered, "Why do you ask, honey?" "'Cause Alison Payne calls you doctor." "Well, I guess I am," I said. "You're a doctor, Daddy," Shannon puzzled, "but nobody ever comes to you." I laughed. "Yeah, I guess you're right, honey." "Well that's alright Daddy," she consoled me. "'Cause you don't even have a kit."

Shannon was right, of course. Some doctor I am. I don't even have a kit. How I wish I did! If I *did* have a kit, I know what I'd carry in it: *Grace!* I'd throw in love, acceptance, forgiveness, and peace. Why? 'Cause that's what we all need to be well, isn't it?

Shannon was right. I don't even have a kit. But I know Someone who does. I have it on good authority this Someone still makes house calls. Anytime, anywhere.

Grace finds us in Christ. Then we grace ourselves.

Self-Forgiveness

Perhaps the first thing we need to forgive ourselves for is not being gods. Only God is sinless. Only God is perfect. We must give up the myth of perfection for the truth of our fallibility. *To accept my imperfection is to position myself as a candidate for grace.* Grace comes to us from the cross of Christ, where God did for us what we cannot do for ourselves: God helped us with our sin problem. In short, God saved us. What

> *To accept my imperfection is to position myself as a candidate for grace.*

God saved us *from* is ourselves. No more self-destruction. No more self-despising. By forgiving us God freed us to forgive ourselves.

To forgive ourselves is to accept ourselves. Self-acceptance always begins outside the self. So does forgiveness. Being made whole by God's forgiveness and acceptance enables us to forgive and accept ourselves. In sum, God's forgiveness leads to self-forgiveness; self-forgiveness leads to self-acceptance; self-acceptance leads to peace.

For most of us trying to forgive ourselves is like learning to walk: it takes awhile! Like God, we want to remove our sins "as far as the east is from the west" (Ps. 103:12 NIV). Yet all previous attempts have blown up on the launching pad. In theory, self-forgiveness may happen in a miracle moment; in practice it may take a long time. The ancient sage, Epictetus, left behind these words of encouragement: "No

176

great thing is created suddenly, any more than a bunch of grapes or figs. If you tell me that you desire a fig, I answer

> When we finally realize that we are spiritually impoverished, and mourn about it, relief is ours at last.

you that there must be time. Let it first blossom, then bear fruit, then ripen."[12] So it is with forgiveness.

"You can't fire a cannon from a canoe," goes an old saying. Forgiveness requires a sure foundation. It does not float in the air like a butterfly to be grabbed. *Among all my patients in the second half of life—that is to say, over thirty-five—,* psychoanalyst Carl Jung revealed, *none of them has been really healed who did not regain his religious outlook.*[13] With the foundation of God's forgiveness in Christ before us, we can address the mechanics of forgiving ourselves.

In order to forgive ourselves, several prerequisites must be in place. We must *not*:

1. ignore our conscience,
2. justify our wrong, or
3. blame others for our behavior.

Rather, as we have seen in earlier chapters, we *must*:

1. accept responsibility for our actions,
2. recognize our guilt,
3. address both the wrong, and our attitude leading to the wrong,
4. repent of our wrongdoing,
5. make restitution when possible,
6. show respect for the victim, and
7. accept God's forgiveness.

We accept God's forgiveness through prayer. Without confession to God and repentance, forgiveness cannot be accepted. Confession to a priest or pastor, a therapist, or a confidante may also help us on our journey toward wholeness. As witnessed in the pages of the New Testament, the healing touch of Jesus reminds us that the cure of souls is best done in community.

The confessional path to forgiveness cannot be bypassed (1 John 1:8–10). But humility without confession is impossible. Admitting a vice is one thing; agreeing with God about the vice, even grieving over it, is another matter altogether. True confession characterized by brokenness and humility leads to repentance. In the Sermon on the Mount, Jesus taught, "Blessed are the poor in spirit, for theirs is the kingdom of heaven" (Matt.

> *Trying on self-forgiveness is a lot like trying on a new pair of shoes: the fit might be a little tight at first. But after a while everything begins to feel better.*

5:3). Recognition of personal spiritual poverty requires humility. Jesus added, "Blessed are those who mourn, for they shall be comforted" (Matt. 5:4). The word translated "blessed" means "happy." The term translated "mourn" refers to a funeral lament. Paradoxically, Jesus was saying that we can be happy when we are sad. When we read Matthew 5:3 and Matthew 5:4 together, the meaning unfolds: *When we finally realize that we are spiritually impoverished, and mourn about it, relief is ours at last.*

Saint Bernard of Clairvaux, a twelfth-century French monk and mystic, called humility "scorn for our own excellence." For Bernard, humility was "a virtue by which man knowing himself exactly as he is, is vile in his own eyes."[14] True humility, it seems, always leads to consciousness of spiritual poverty, which in turn leads to confession and repentance. Catharsis follows.

Trying on self-forgiveness is a lot like trying on a new pair of shoes: the fit might be a little tight at first. But after a while everything begins to feel better.

Ten ingredients in the recipe for forgiveness were identified in chapter 6. I choose to refer to concepts as ingredients rather than as steps, since even though a list is given, no particular order is suggested. Many of the same principles involved in forgiving others apply to self-forgiveness as well. So how do we forgive ourselves? We forgive ourselves: (1) slowly, (2) humanly, (3) divinely, (4) as we limit the load, (5) by taking appropriate action to create new realities, (6) by *praying* (for which there is *absolutely NO* substitute!), (7) by living Christianly (which begins the process of transforming our self-image), and (8) *through prayer, prayer,* and *more prayer.* With prayer, the impossible becomes possible.

> Unless we exchange our fig leaves of self-contempt for skins of grace, life is unbearable.

Judas betrayed Jesus. So did Peter. Both suffered a massive attack of guilt, which threw each man into spiritual cardiac arrest. Self-hatred struck like a stroke. Each disciple required immediate intensive care. Only one thing could restore these men to spiritual health: forgiveness! No other medicine would do. Each required forgiveness from Christ and self. One man became well; the other did not. One experienced forgiveness; the other did not. One thrived; the other committed suicide.

When, like Judas and Peter, we betray loved ones, the thread of our lives pulls and soon unravels. We stand naked in our shame. Unless we exchange our fig leaves of self-contempt for skins of grace, life is unbearable. Ultimately the difference between accepting and not accepting God's forgiveness and forgiveness for self is the difference between life and death. The examples of Peter and Judas show us this all too clearly. While we cheer for Simon Peter, we weep for Judas. If only Judas had waited. Surely the resurrected Christ would have come to him as he did to Peter. If Judas had only accepted Christ's forgiveness, he wouldn't have committed suicide. If he had found it possible to pray, "Lord, please forgive me, and help me to forgive myself," his fate might have been different.

Self-Love

The son of a rabbi went to worship on the Sabbath in a nearby village. Upon his return, his family asked, "Well, did they do anything different from what we do here?" "Yes, of course," said the son. "Then what was the lesson?" "Love thy enemy as thyself." "So, it's the same as we say. And how is it you learned something else?" "They taught me to love the enemy within myself."[15]

Hmmm . . . novel idea, that one; loving the *internal*, not the external, enemy. Of course we should love all our enemies. Jesus taught that. "Love your enemies," he said (Matt. 5:44 NIV). Jesus also taught us to love our neighbor as ourselves, while apparently assuming that we would, in fact, love ourselves. Easier said than done. Many of us come closer to despising ourselves than loving ourselves. Sometimes our own worst enemy *is* ourselves. As the cartoon figure Pogo once said, "We have met the enemy and the enemy is us." Is it really possible to love the enemy within us? Isn't the hardest person of all to love and forgive our self?

Saint Bernard of Clairvaux contemplated what we might call a ladder of spiritual maturity. He said those on the lowest rung *love self for self's sake*. Love for self's sake is essentially an infantile stage of self-centered existence. Those on the second rung of the ladder *love God for self's sake*. These folk realize that it is in their best interest to love the Creator and Judge of all. Those ascending to the third step *love God for God's sake*. These individuals are the pure of heart. They are not in a relationship with God for what they can get out of it. Instead they simply love God for who God is. These are the spiritual giants, the models for the rest of us.[16]

To my surprise, Bernard includes a final rung on his ladder of spiritual development. The idea that there could be a form of maturation higher than loving God unconditionally is suspect for most of us. After all, isn't arriving at the third level of the ladder an ascension to the heights of divine love itself? Could any form of love possibly be higher? Bernard suggests so. According to Bernard, the *highest* form of love in the universe is *love of self for God's sake!*[17]

When we think long and hard about his stages of love, Bernard's conviction makes sense. Who is harder to love than ourselves? We are not talking about narcissism here but something altogether different. Spiritual love differs radically from selfish love. To love ourselves for God's sake is to invite God into the care for our soul. Only those willing to dance with God will ever reach this dance floor.

I would amend Bernard's ladder to include our relationship with others. The second and third levels respectively would read "Love of God *and others* for self's sake," and "Love of God *and others* for their sakes." Other than those changes, I am persuaded by Bernard's argument. We sin, not because we love ourselves too much, but because we do not love ourselves enough. If we really loved ourselves like God loves us, wouldn't all our choices serve our highest good? Isn't Jesus the model here?

Will any of us reach this zenith of spirituality? Perhaps. I do not believe many of us will. Most of us will continue to struggle. I count myself in that number. Did Bernard reach the highest level of spiritual maturity? I'll let him speak for himself: "I do not know whether it is possible for anyone to arrive during his earthly life at the fourth degree in which man loves himself only for the sake of God." Then he adds, "As for myself, I do not think it is possible in this world."[18]

Never Perfect

When Jesus calls us by name and says, "Come to Me, all who are weary and heavy-laden, and I will give you rest. . . . you will find rest for your souls" (Matt. 11:28–29), he is scratching where I itch. If Jesus is passing out grace, I'm standing in the handout line.

In his book *Blessing: Giving the Gift of Power*, Myron Madden claims, "The incarnation is not so much a story about a perfect human as a story showing it is perfectly all right to

> *An African greeting begins, "Are you well?"*
> *The response comes, "I am if you are."*

be human."[19] None of us will ever be perfect. It's okay to admit that. "You got burdens; I got burdens; all God's chillun' got burdens." The one burden none of us has to carry is the burden of infallibility. We can lay that burden down right now, down by the riverside.

An African greeting begins, "Are you well?" The response comes, "I am if you are." What intimacy! What community! What love! The beauty, goodness, and truth of that salutation contains healing power. Perhaps none of us is completely well. But together we travel, leaving no child of God behind.

"Peace be with you," Jesus said to us. "As the Father has sent Me, I also send you" (John 20:21). So it is we are commissioned to help others. As the prophet Isaiah reminds us, our vision is first upward, then inward, and finally outward (Isaiah 6). The movement is toward missions. We move from self-absorption to other-centeredness. We lose ourselves in caring for others. We wait only for cleansing, not perfection. As Henri Nouwen put it, our call is to be wounded healers.

Conclusion

I saiah of old prophesied,

> Do you not know? Have you not heard?
> The Everlasting God, the LORD, the Creator of the
> ends of the earth
> . . . gives strength to the weary . . .
> Those who wait for the LORD
>   will gain new strength;
>   they will mount up with wings like eagles,
>   they will run and not get tired,
>   they will walk and not become weary.

Isaiah 40:28–29, 31

In seeking to bring his oratorical charge to a climax, shouldn't the prophet have reversed his sequence of metaphor? Is not moving from soaring with eagles, to running, then walking anticlimatic? At first it appears so. Upon reflection, however, Isaiah's promise of strength from God saves its greatest hope until last. There are days of sunshine and blue skies when living is easy. On those days we "mount up with wings like eagles." Then there are those much tougher times when to be able to "run and not get tired" is a gift from God. Ah, but the day comes when the world caves in on top of us, when we enter "the dark night of the soul," when we honestly do not know if we can make it. The Lord's greatest gift of grace is reserved for this hour. When it is all we can do to put one foot in front of the other, those who wait upon the Lord "will gain new strength," "they will walk and not become weary."

Jacob and Esau were twins. Since Esau came into the world first, according to the custom of ancient Israel, he was entitled to the birthright and blessing of his father, Isaac. This entitlement meant Esau would receive a double portion of the inheritance from his father's estate. In addition his father's formal pronouncement of blessing would ensure Esau power to prosper. Jacob, whose name means "heel holder," was a highly ambitious, shrewd deceiver, whose legend as an unsavory character can be traced all the way back to childbirth. There Jacob appeared to be holding his brother back by the heel in order to become

> *The Good Book says it's okay to limp.*

the firstborn. Later in life, using cunning, crass lies, and deception, he seized from his brother both the birthright and the blessing. Their blind, old father, Isaac, lamented to Esau, "Your brother came deceitfully and has taken away your blessing." Esau seethed, "'Is he not rightly named Jacob, for he has supplanted me these two times? He took away my birthright, and behold, now he has taken away my blessing.' . . . So Esau lifted his voice and wept" (Gen. 27:35–36, 38).

So what happens next? "Esau bore a grudge against Jacob because of the blessing with which his father had blessed him; and Esau said to himself, 'The days of mourning for my father are near; then I will kill my brother Jacob'" (Gen. 27:41). Learning of his brother's plan, Jacob flees. Coming home years later, Jacob is greatly afraid and distressed when he learns that Esau is rushing out to meet him with four hundred men. Jacob crosses the river Jabbok and is all alone. In a highly enigmatic episode, a mysterious being wrestles with Jacob all through the night until daybreak.

When he saw that he had not prevailed against him (Jacob), he touched the socket of his thigh; so the socket of Jacob's thigh was dislocated while he wrestled with him. Then he said, "Let me go, for the dawn is breaking." But he said, "I will not let you go unless you bless me." So he said to him, "What is your name?" And he said, "Jacob." He said, "Your name shall no longer be Jacob, but Israel; for you have striven with God and with men and have prevailed."...And he blessed him there. So Jacob named the place Peniel, for he said, "I have seen God face to face, yet my life has been preserved."

Genesis 32:25–30

From this point onward, Jacob was a changed person. No longer was he the "heel holder," but he was given the name Israel, meaning "prince of God," or "one who strives with God." He was reconciled to his brother, then rose to great heights for God, becoming the famed father of the twelve tribes of Israel.

The story of Jacob's forgiveness and reconciliation to God, brother, and self concludes with a telling verse:

Now the sun rose upon him just as he crossed over Penuel, and he was *limping* on his thigh.

Genesis 32:31, italics mine

When we suffer the pain and anguish of broken relationships, guilt, and fear, God comes to us down by the river Jabbok. There, like Jacob, we wrestle with God, refusing to let go until we receive the blessing of a new name. We are no longer called "Unforgiven" but "*Forgiven.*"

As we continue on our journey home, we may not arrive on wings of eagles, nor with the fleet-footed. It may well be all we can do to enter the gates of heaven limping. But that's okay. The Good Book says it's okay to limp, in our struggle to be *set free by forgiveness*.

Notes

Introduction

1. "Child Kidnapper Finds Jesus from Victim's Witness," *The Baptist Record,* July 27, 2000, 12; George Henson, "San Marcos Teacher Learned to Forgive through His Own Trauma," *Baptist Standard,* November 26, 2001, 1.

Chapter 1 Understanding Our Dark Side

1. Carl Jung, *The Archetypes and the Collective Unconscious* (Princeton, NJ: Princeton University Press, 1969), 284.

2. Anthony Stevens, *Archetype: A Natural History of the Self* (New York: William Morrow, 1982), 210–43.

3. William A. Miller, *Make Friends with Your Shadow* (Minneapolis: Augsburg, 1981), 78.

4. William McGuire, ed., *The Collected Works of Carl Jung* (Princeton, NJ: Princeton University Press, 1980), Cw 13, par. 335.

5. Mark Water, ed., *The New Encyclopedia of Christian Quotations* (Grand Rapids: Baker Books, 2000), 636.

Chapter 2 Understanding Being Sinned Against

1. Alex Haley, *The Autobiography of Malcolm X* (New York: Ballantine Books, 1965), 1–3.

2. Maria Henson, "Daisy Bates Honored as Woman of Impact," *Arkansas Gazette,* February 9, 1989, 1A.

3. Ibid.

4. John Powell, *Why Am I Afraid to Love* (Niles, IL: Argus, 1972), 115–16.

5. Ibid., 114, 116.

6. Connie Zweig and Jeremiah Abrams, eds., *Meeting the Shadow: The Hidden Power of the Dark Side of Human Nature* (New York: G. P. Putnam's Sons, 1991), 194.

Chapter 3 Guilt and Shame

1. Linda Storm, *Karla Faye Tucker Set Free* (Colorado Springs: Shaw, 2000), 45.

2. Ibid., 147.

3. Dietrich Bonhoeffer, *The Cost of Discipleship* (New York: Macmillan, 1963), 324–25.

Chapter 4 What Is Forgiveness?

1. Jimmy Lee Gray's story was related to me orally in December 1985 by Parchman (Mississippi) State Penitentiary voluntary chaplain Tommy Ellis.

2. Robert L. Short, *The Parables of Peanuts* (New York: Harper & Row, 1968), 46–47.

3. Martin Luther King Jr., *Why We Can't Wait* (New York: Mentor, New American Library, Inc., 1964), 81.

4. Erich Fromm, *The Art of Loving* (New York: Perennial Library, Harper & Row, 1956), 8.

5. Jean-Paul Sartre, *No Exit, and Three Other Plays* (New York: Vintage Books, 1949), 47.

6. Clyde E. Fant Jr. and William M. Pinson Jr., eds., *20 Centuries of Great Preaching*, vol. 12 (Waco: Word Books, 1971), 354.

7. Ibid., 356.

Chapter 5 Why Forgive?

1. Louis Fischer, *The Life of Mahatma Gandhi* (New York: Harper & Row, 1983), 77.

2. Elie Wiesel, *The Night Trilogy* (New York: Noonday Press, 1985), 38, 48.

3. Richard B. Hays, *The Moral Vision of the New Testament* (New York: HarperSanFrancisco, 1996), 27.

4. Lance Morrow, "Why Forgive? The Pope Pardons the Gunman," *Time*, January 9, 1984, 29.

5. Caroline J. Simon, "Which Way to Forgiveness?" *Christian Reflection*, Fall 2001, 85.

6. Tim Noel, "The Gospel According to *Gunsmoke*," *Proclaim*, April, May, June, 1990, 5.

7. Clayton Bellamy, "Former KKK Leader Now Fighting Racism," *Waco Tribune-Herald*, June 15, 2002, 6D.

8. Mark Water, ed., *The New Encyclopedia of Christian Quotations* (Grand Rapids: Baker Books, 2000), 375.

9. David J. Brewer, ed., *The World's Best Orations* (Chicago: Kaiser, 1923), 333.

Chapter 6 How Do We Forgive?

1. Storm, *Karla Faye Tucker Set Free*, 50–51.

2. T. B. Maston, *Why Live the Christian Life?* (Nashville: Thomas Nelson, 1974), 142.

3. W. E. Vine, *An Expository Dictionary of New Testament Words*, vol. 3 (Westwood, NJ: Fleming H. Revell Company, 1966), s.v. "Agapao," 21.

4. William James, *The Principles of Psychology* (Cambridge: Harvard University Press, 1983), 1162–63.

5. Donald Phillips, *Lincoln on Leadership* (New York: Warner Books, 1992), 66.

6. Ibid., 29–31.

7. Ibid., 62.

Chapter 7 Forgiveness from God

1. Mark Water, ed., *The New Encyclopedia of Christian Quotations* (Grand Rapids: Baker Books, 2000), 839.

2. Desmond Tutu, *No Future without Forgiveness* (New York: Doubleday, 1999), 272.

3. Kenneth L. Woodward, "Pick-and-Choose Christianity," *Newsweek*, September, 19, 1983, 82.

4. Ronald J. Sider, *Rich Christians in an Age of Hunger* (Nashville: Word Publishing, 1997), 2.

5. George Gallup Jr. and D. Michael Lindsay, *Surveying the Religious Landscape: Trends in U.S. Beliefs* (Harrisburg, PA: Morehouse, 1999), 101–2.

6. Karl Barth, *Deliverance to the Captives* (New York: Harper & Brothers, 1961), 135.

7. Edward Connery Lathem, ed., *The Poetry of Robert Frost* (New York: Holt, Rinehart and Winston, 1967), 105.

8. Flannery O'Conner, *Wise Blood* (New York: Signet Books, 1962), 60–68, 109–26.

Chapter 8 Forgiveness for God

1. Lewis Smedes, *Forgive and Forget* (San Francisco: Harper & Row, 1984), 82.

2. Tom J. Logue, *God, Could You Talk a Little Louder?* (Little Rock: Kent Popular Press, 1990), 65.

3. Elie Wiesel, *The Trial of God* (New York: Schocken Press, 1979), 43, 125.

4. Jurgen Moltmann, *The Crucified God* (San Francisco: Harper & Row, 1974), 4.

5. Ibid., 222.

6. Feodor Dostoyevsky, *Brothers Karamozov* (New York: Penguin Books, 1983), 278.

7. Robert L. Short, *The Parables of Peanuts* (New York: Harper & Row, 1968), 124.

8. Archibald Macleish, *J.B.* (Boston: Houghton Mifflin, 1956), 109–11, 151.

Chapter 9 Forgiveness for Others

1. Thomas Long, "To Err Is Human; To Forgive . . . ?" *Christian Reflection* (Fall 2001): 34.

2. Corrie ten Boom, *The Hiding Place* (Carmel, NY: Guideposts, 1971), 215.

3. Gallup poll statistics are from 1988 as quoted in Everett L. Worthington Jr., ed., *Dimensions of Forgiveness: Psychological Research & Theological Perspectives* (Philadelphia: Templeton Foundation Press, 1998), 277–78.

4. "Forgiving Mother Wants Son's Slayer to Go Free," *USA Today*, December 5, 1986.

5. Quoted in Zweig and Abrams, *Meeting the Shadow*, iv.
6. Quoted in ibid., 62.
7. Simon Wiesenthal, *The Sunflower* (New York: Schocken Press, 1976), 46.
8. Elisabeth Kübler-Ross, *On Death and Dying* (New York: Macmillan, 1969), 38–137.

Chapter 10 Forgiveness for Self

1. Edwin Arlington Robinson, "Richard Cory," *Collected Poems*, with an introduction by John Drinkwater (London: Cecil Palmer, 1922): 82, http://eir.library.utoronto.ca/rpo/display/poem1735.html. Poem was first published 1890–1897 and is in the public domain.
2. Mark Water, ed., *The New Encyclopedia of Christian Quotations* (Grand Rapids: Baker Books, 2000), 160.
3. Ibid.
4. M. Scott Peck, *People of the Lie: The Hope for Healing Human Evil* (New York: Simon and Schuster, 1983), 69.
5. M. Scott Peck, *The Road Less Traveled: A New Psychology of Love, Traditional Values and Spiritual Growth* (New York: Simon and Schuster, 1978), 278.
6. Kathleen W., ed., *12 Steps to Freedom: A Recovery Workbook* (Freedom, CA: Crossing Press, 1991), 8–138.
7. Paul Tournier, *Guilt and Grace* (New York: Harper & Row, 1962), 185.
8. Dallas Willard, *The Divine Conspiracy* (San Francisco: HarperSanFrancisco, 1966), 43.
9. Peck, *The Road Less Traveled*, 307.
10. Philip Yancey, *What's So Amazing about Grace?* (Grand Rapids: Zondervan Publishing House, 1997), 11.
11. Miller, *Make Friends with Your Shadow*, 134.
12. Kathleen W., ed., *12 Steps to Freedom*, 27.
13. Wayne G. Rollins, *Jung and the Bible* (Atlanta: John Knox Press, 1983), 119.
14. Leon Cristiani, *St. Bernard of Clairvaux* (Boston: St. Paul Editions, 1983), 151.
15. Zweig and Abrams, *Meeting the Shadow*, 190.
16. Cristiani, *St. Bernard of Clairvaux*, 153–54.
17. Ibid., 154.
18. Ibid.
19. Myron Madden, *Blessing: Giving the Gift of Power* (Nashville: Broadman, 1988), 77.

Randall O'Brien is professor and chair of the department of religion at Baylor University and visiting professor of law in the Baylor Law School. He has pastored several churches and is the author of three books and more than seventy articles. The recipient of several outstanding professor awards, he speaks widely at churches, conferences, and on college campuses.